DATE			

STUDIES IN AFRICAN AMERICAN HISTORY AND CULTURE

edited by
GRAHAM HODGES
COLGATE UNIVERSITY

A GARLAND SERIES

BESSIE COLEMAN

THE BROWNSKIN LADY BIRD

ELIZABETH AMELIA HADLEY FREYDBERG

GARLAND PUBLISHING, INC.
NEW YORK & LONDON / 1994

Library of Congress Cataloging-in-Publication Data

Freydberg, Elizabeth Hadley.
   Bessie Coleman, the brownskin lady bird / Elizabeth Amelia
Hadley Freydberg.
       p.   cm. — (Studies in African American history and culture)
   Includes bibliographical references and index.
   ISBN 0–8153–1461–2 (alk. paper)
       1. Coleman, Bessie, 1896–1926.   2. Afro-American air pilots—
Biography.   3. Women air pilots—United States—Biography.
I. Title. II. Series.
TL540.C646F74   1994
629.13'092—dc20
[B]   93–44882
                                                                        CIP

Printed on acid-free, 250-year-life paper
Manufactured in the United States of America

For Malika

In Loving Memory of

Kathleen Collins
(1942-1988)

Hazel Joan Bryant
(1939-1983)

Janet Harmon Bragg
(1907-1993)

Women who Believed

Contents

Illustrations

Bessie Coleman*
by Ross D. Brown

If your imagination is good you can fancy a dauntless brownskin Ladybird, using her aeroplane for a fountain pen, the exhaust of smoke for ink, and God's blue sky for her paper.

That's brave little Bessie Coleman writing her name across the sky in a sensational aerial act of spectacular penmanship.

She was blessed with the power of perseverance, and walked many long miles each day to learn, and teach her people how to fly. She was fearless as Franklin, as noble as Newton, as brave as Bruno, and as wonderful as Wright.

She knew that tireless wings were faster than tender feet. She loved the music of the motor and the purr of the propeller; she disputed with the Eagle and broke his brilliant record.

She believed in service rather than sentiment, she loved performance better than pleasure, she gave exhibitions and not excuses. She pushed her silver wings thru [sic] the clefts of the lazy clouds and brought back a wonderful story of the stars.

She flew over the Royal Palace, encircled the Eifel [sic] Tower, and spanned the English Channel.

The whole world was her country, she flew all flags and examined all facts, and learned that people are pitiful who have no power.

She performed while her people prayed, she dared while they danced, she soared while they slept.

She asked Negro business men to pool their funds and help to motorize the sky. She received no reply, and was forced to consider others who took an interest in her cause.

She had a vision and saw great airships crossing Seas and bombing helpless humanity; she fought and flew ahead of her time and was greatly misunderstood.

She knew the poverty of the past, the possibilities of the present, and the forces of the future.

She knew a bird was faster than a buggy, that winging was better than walking, and that aviation was greater than ignorance.

The most scientific of her sex, the most courageous of her color, the most progressive of her people.

If she had a fault it was in the lack of fear.

She liked distance and laughed at danger; she was a patient pioneer that loved adventure and knew the price of progress.

She was thrilling thousands at Jacksonville when the fatal crash came. The gears jammed, something went wrong and brave Bessie Coleman was hurled to instant death.

People who could have promoted her program while she lived, wept and worshipped her after she died.

I saw the machine from which she fell; twisted wires burnt metal and broken wheels. I thought of the countries she crossed, I thought of the thousands she thrilled, and I thought of the price she paid for being a vigilant veteran and teaching the scheme of the sky.

Brave little Bessie Coleman fought with a stout heart and died beneath broken wings; she tried to awaken her people, then reported back to God and wore her purple plume to heaven.

*Ross D. Brown, *Watching My Race Go By. Feats, Facts, and Faults Of the Negro Race,* 2nd Edition, *The Chicago Whip*, February 28, 1931:31-32. Note: Epigraphs at the beginning of each chapter are lines from this poem except for Chapter II.

BESSIE COLEMAN

THE RACE'S ONLY

AVIATRIX

**WILL MAKE HER INITIAL
LOCAL FLIGHT AT**

CHECKERBOARD AIRDROME

SUNDAY, OCT. 15

3 P. M. SHARP

DIRECTIONS

METROPOLITAN "L"—Garfield Park to Forest Park station; motor bus to field.

ALTO ROUTE— West on Jackson Blvd. to Desplaines Ave., south to Roosevelt Road, west three blocks to Checkerboard Airdrome.

SEE THIS DAREDEVIL AVIATRIX

IN HER

HAIR-RAISING STUNTS

Including French Nungesser Take-off, Spanish Berta Costa Climb, American Curtis-McMullen Turn, Eddie Rickenbacker Straighten-up, Richtofen German Glide, Ralph C. Diggins Landing. Presentation of Honor Flag to 8th Ill. Infantry. Wing Walking and Parachute Jumps

FOUR SEPARATE FLIGHTS

AND SPECIAL PASSENGER CARRYING

Admission: Children, 25 Cents. Adults, $1.00

1. Coleman Barnstorming Advertisement as it appeared in
The Chicago Defender Saturday, 14 October 1922

Preface

I was first introduced to the subject of African American aviatrixes in 1984 by the late Kathleen Collins (1943-1988), filmmaker, director, playwright, and professor. Collins had been commissioned by the late Hazel Joan Bryant (1939-1983), an off-Broadway producer and executive director of the Richard Allen Center for Culture and Art, to write a playscript about African American women pilots. Dr. Phyllis Klotman introduced me to Kathleen Collins, who after having read my "Annotated Bibliography on Black Catholics in the United States," hired me in 1984 to do the research for her play and filmscript. Bryant died shortly after providing Collins with a check which she turned over to me to begin research on the project. During our initial meeting at the home of Dr. Phyllis Klotman, Collins provided me with a list of women believed to be, or associated with African American aviatrixes.

My first assignment on Collins' 1984 project was to assemble as much information on African American aviatrixes into what Collins referred to as a "treatment" for her to write the scripts. This is a chronological listing of information developed from answers to her specific questions regarding the social, political, and cultural milieux of the period to be represented. After several conferences Collins and I agreed to focus on Bessie Coleman because I had by now, acquired information initiated by a micro-fische of newspaper clippings received from Elizabeth Gubert, then Head Librarian of the Schomburg Center for Research in Black Culture at the New York Public Library, suggesting that Coleman may have been the pioneering source of Black American involvement in aviation. Collins included my completed overview on "The Life and Times of Bessie Coleman" to develop her "treatment" which she presented to the New York National Endowment for the Humanities in pursuit of financial assistance for scripting the play and film. It was this chronological overview that enabled me to recognize a direct correlation between socio-political ideologies and the cultural activities pursued by American people during the late nineteenth and early twentieth centuries. Collins completed her "fictional meditation" entitled *Only the Sky Is Free* (1986), and during one of our frequent "brainstorming" discussions, encouraged me to develop my remaining research materials into a scholarly thesis on how these institutions influenced each other and consequently guided (directly or indirectly) the cultural activities of Bessie Coleman.

My research was frequently encumbered by meager finances that prevented me from traveling to interviews and archives that were vital to my research. As a result, I had to depend on long-distance telephone interviews and await answers to my letters of inquiry. This meant that I was often at the mercy of temperamental individuals, who did not share my enthusiasm regarding the research. This approach retarded my work because I had to always follow-up letters with telephone calls and vice-versa. With limited financial resources, I had to employ much ingenuity in procuring research information nationally. To this end, Kathleen Collins provided me with "seed" money in 1984, her long distance telephone card for national telephone interviews, and a round-trip ticket to Chicago in January 1985, making it possible for me to conduct my prearranged interviews with the late Enoch Waters (1910-1987), former editor of the *Chicago Defender* and co-founder of a civilian aviation school for Black Americans in Chicago. Although bedridden and ill, in 1985, Waters graciously permitted me to read his chapter "Little Air Show Becomes A National Crusade," from the galleys of his then unpublished book, *American Diary: A Personal History of the Black Press* (1987), onto audiotape. Marion Coleman, niece of Bessie Coleman, Janyce Givens, president of the Bessie Coleman Aviators, and Rufus Hunt, pilot and aviation historian all graciously shared their time, knowledge and wisdom with me during interviews. Dr. Herman Hudson assisted me in purchasing the appropriate recording mechanisms for connection to my home telephone to conduct long-distance interviews. My former student Laura Smith researched and collected documentation on Bessie Coleman's educational background while on a trip to Oklahoma in 1985. Collins' former inlaws, Marion Coleman, and Jo Enne Jennings provided room and board for me and my daughter during my interviews in Chicago.

My trip to Chicago in January 1985, coincided with the gala opening of the "Black Wings Exhibit" at the Museum of Space and Science in Chicago. Although we had no invitation to this "black tie" affair, Collins and I skillfully managed to gain admission where I recorded the names of the guests, who were primarily African American aviatrixes and aviators. They were identified by large brass name tags worn on their lapels or collars. It was at this event that I first met the late Janet Harmon Bragg and Ida Van-Smith whose oral histories of the socio-political climate have proven to be invaluable in the advancement of my research; and who both became lasting friends.

Finally, in 1992 during a flight back from Paris where I had given a paper on Bessie Coleman, Dr. Randall K. Burkett, voluntarily granted me the use of his unpublished essay entitled "The Baptist Church in the Years of Crisis: J.C. Austin and Pilgrim Baptist Church, 1926-50," which establishes that Reverend Austin had backed Coleman and was committed to supporting African American aviators in Chicago.

Acknowledgments

It has been my good fortune to have had the encouragement, commentary, and support of mentors, colleagues, friends and librarians in the preparation of this manuscript. Consequently, by the time this book was completed these categories had blurred; all had become friends. My work on Bessie Coleman began as a challenge from the late Kathleen Collins, educator, filmmaker, playwright and author; and took flight with the reminisces of the women who fly: the late Janet Harmon Bragg, aviatrix; the late Willa Brown, aviatrix; Mary Oglesby, aviatrix and Major in the Indiana Civil Air Patrol; and Ida Van Smith, aviatrix and founder of the Ida Van Smith Flight Clubs. My interviews with these women and further research were made possible by the Support Fund for Black and Hispanic Faculty in 1990 and a 1991 Faculty Development Grant from Northeastern University.

A very special thank you to the following for their continued faith in the importance of this work to future generations: Dr. Frances Stubbs, Dr. Charles Nero, Eileen Hayes, Dr. Cheryl Keyes, Audrey Aduana, Patricia Powell, Teresa Langle, William C. Lowe, Julia Lowe, Dr. Joy James, Dr. Ruth Farmer, Dr. Kim Vaz, Dr. Randall K. Burkett, Dr. Phyllis Klotman, Dr. Clark White, Dr. Jeanne Phoenix Laurel, Dr. Portia K. Maultsby, Dr. Gloria Gibson-Hudson, Dr. Herman Hudson, Renita Martin, Nadine Jones, Michéle Battle, Robin White, Patricia Orr, Terri Ward-Nelson, Tia Juana Malone and Robert McKenzie.

A special acknowledgment must be extended to the many librarians and archivists who often go unrecognized, but who have the power to make or break a manuscript. My investigation into the life of Bessie Coleman would have been seriously deficient if not for the indefatigable assistance of the late Wilmer Baatz, African American Studies Librarian, Indiana University; Elizabeth Gubert, Head Librarian Schomburg Center for Research in Black Culture, New York Public Library; Rosalind Savage, Librarian at the Black Heritage Center at Langston University in Oklahoma in 1987, now Head Librarian of the African American Institute, Northeastern University; Damaris N'anga, Humanities Librarian, Kenyatta University, Nairobi Kenya; Rhonda Stone, Indiana University; Dorothy Ann Washington, Chief Technical Processes Librarian, Bethune-Cookman College; and Mary Ann Pere, Reference Librarian, American Center Library, at the American Cultural Center, Nairobi Kenya, East Africa; and Dr. Walter Hill, National Archives.

My sincerest gratitude is extended to Dr. Patrick Manning, and Dr. Jacqueline Goggin, friends and colleagues who meticulously read my manuscript and provided me with notes and suggestions to enhance it. My heartfelt appreciation to Joanna Banks, friend and educator at the Anacostia Museum for a critical reading of the manuscript and for nurturing mind and spirit; and finally to Malika Hadley Freydberg, a constant reminder that the stories of our ancestors are indispensable foundations for those yet to arrive.

2. Bessie Coleman's Aviation License from the Fèdèration Aèronitique Internationale. *Courtesy of Elizabeth Hadley Freydberg*

3. Bessie Coleman with Airplane and Car. *Courtesy of The New York Public Library Schomburg Center for Research in Black Culture.*

COMING SOON!

D. IRELAND THOMAS

PRESENTS

MISS BESSIE COLEMAN

The Only Colored Girl Aviatrix In The World.

In Person and on the Screen, showing her flights in Europe and America and her accident while flying in California.

Being impossible to fly in every City or Town, Miss Coleman is bringing her flights to you in Motion Pictures and appearing in person at every showing. Join the mighty throng and see the idol of the race; greet her. Shake her hand as she has blazed a new trail for the race. Come early as every one will be there to see the little girl who has the nerve to fly.

After flying in Europe, Miss Coleman has made successful flights in New York, Columbus, Ohio, Los Angeles, Cal., Memphis, Tenn., Etc.

4. Handbill Announcing Coleman's National Touring with Documentary Film footage of her American and European Flights. *Courtesy of Phyllis Rauch Klotman and the Black Film Center Archives, Indian aUniversity/Bloomington.*

Bessie Coleman

I

Introduction

If your imagination is good you can fancy a dauntless brownskin Ladybird, using her aeroplane [sic] for a fountain pen, the exhaust of smoke for ink, and God's blue sky for her paper. That's brave little Bessie Coleman writing her name across the sky in a sensational aerial act of spectacular penmanship.

Ross D. Brown

The purpose of this investigation is to introduce Bessie Coleman (1896-1926) into the study of popular culture while emphasizing that culture as an integral component to the study of American popular entertainment. Coleman was a pioneer in American aviation during its infancy. Her career choices and adaptations were in direct correlation to the transformation of American society in general, and to entertainment in particular. Entertainment was one avenue by which African Americans could enter mainstream America, and Coleman made an attempt to embrace at least three significant forms of entertainment popular during the early twentieth century--melodrama, barnstorming and film.

Coleman's initial pursuit of a formal education in aviation was met with rejection from the administrations of newly-established aviation schools in the United States because she was an African American woman. These schools were conforming to federal jurisdiction of Jim Crow laws that stipulated separation between the races. Coleman temporarily eluded this discrimination by registering in an aviation school located in France in 1920. Upon completion of her program of study, she received the first international pilot's license administered to an American aviator. Coleman returned to the United States from France in 1921, and attempted to enlist in a commercial career in aviation, but she again learned that her immediate dream would not meet fruition because African Americans and women were excluded from commercial aviation. Undaunted, Coleman immediately went back to France and specialized in parachuting and stunt flying. This time she returned to the United States as a "Barnstormer."

The earliest barnstormers in aviation were former military men who performed acrobatics with their planes in the air, and who for a small fee, took adventurous people for airplane rides.[1] Eventually they were anyone who could afford to purchase one of the surplus airplanes made available to the public at the end of World War I. Since there were no aviation regulations at the time, one did not have to know how to fly in order to purchase and operate an airplane. In fact, regulations were devised because the lives of pilots, spectators and innocent bystanders became increasingly endangered with the proliferation of inexperienced people in the air.[2]

Coleman traveled throughout the United States performing in air shows. After she received recognition as a top-flight barnstormer from predominantly white audiences and press in the Northern regions, she eventually concentrated her performances in the South where her audiences were primarily African American. Many of her Southern appearances were at circuses, carnivals and fairs on the Theatre Owners Booking Association (T.O.B.A.) circuit that also included black theatres where documentary film footage of Coleman's achievements were shown between acts.[3] She lectured at African American schools and churches in an attempt to encourage African Americans to become involved in aviation, and to raise money to launch an aviation training school for African American people in the United States. During an era in United States history when African Americans were excluded both legally and extralegally from most American institutions, segregation laws did not apply to air travel. In fact, this was the only division in American public transportation without segregation laws.[4] C. Vann Woodward asserts that:

> The arrival of the age of air transportation appears to have put a strain upon the ingenuity of the Jim Crow lawmakers. Even to the orthodox there was doubtless something slightly incongruous about requiring a Jim Crow compartment on a transcontinental plane, or one that did not touch the ground between New York and Miami. No Jim Crow law has been found that applies to passengers while they are in the air. So long as they were upon the ground, however, they were still subject to Jim Crow jurisdiction.[5]

This information provides a plausible motive for Coleman's choice of aviation as one vehicle for African Americans to enter mainstream America. Since entertainment was another, her combination of the two, seemed destined to carry her objective to fruition.

Coleman was a woman who was unafraid to perform daring feats, of parachuting, wing walking, and figure eights in the air, when the general consensus in the aviation community was that African Americans were mentally incapable of flying an airplane.[6] This attitude prevailed and was manifested in *defacto* and *dejure* discriminatory practices in United States civilian and military aviation institutions from the apex of aviation during the 1920s, up until President Harry Truman signed a bill that technically terminated segregation in all branches of the armed forces in 1948.[7] Although Coleman's contribution was made in entertainment and not in the military, she is considered by some persons to have been the catalyst for African American involvement in aviation during World War II. The late Janet Harmon Bragg (née Waterford) and Phillip Hart surmised that Coleman's daring bolstered the courage of men who, after observing her, took to the air—if a woman could do it so could they.[8]

Bessie Coleman was unique in several ways. First, her trip to France was financed by two African American philanthropists—Robert Abbott, the renowned founder and editor of the *Chicago Defender,* and Jesse Binga, founder and president of one of the most prestigious banks in Chicago throughout the 1920s. Her activities were framed by an era now referred to as the Harlem Renaissance; the era of the "New Negro." This was a period during which philosopher Alain Locke declared in the theme piece for the Harlem Renaissance *The New Negro* (1925), that after fifty years of freedom it was time for America to view the New Negro as an intelligent person seeking recognition through achievement in education, art, sciences, and other realms of American life just as their white counterparts because:

> The day of 'aunties,' 'uncles,' and 'mammies' is equally gone. Uncle Tom and Sambo have passed on, and even the 'Colonel' and 'George' play barnstorm rôles [sic] from which they escape with relief when the public spotlight is off. The popular melodrama has about played itself out, and it is time to scrap the fictions, garret the bogeys and settle down to a realistic facing of facts.[9]

Many African Americans seeking recognition through aesthetic channels however, turned primarily to white philanthropists for financial backing in order to produce authentic African American cultural works. Artists Langston Hughes and Zora Neale Hurston, among others, readily accepted this financial assistance at first, but inevitably found their artistic visions compromised or restricted by the dictates of their white patrons. Those who did not rely directly upon white patrons nevertheless sought contacts and connections through salons sponsored by whites like Carl Van Vechten and Nancy Cunard, whose motives seemed at times to be tinged with voyeurism or outright condescension.[10] Coleman's insistence on African American resources implies that she was aware of the dangers of becoming a faddish object of philanthropic interest, to be discontinued when the Negro was no longer in vogue.

Secondly, Bessie Coleman did not become an expatriate in spite of the opposition directed at her dream. Several African Americans for example, Josephine Baker, Claude McKay, Eugene Jacques Bullard, the world's first African American combat aviator, and others became expatriates to escape racism and to pursue the artistic calling of their souls.[11] Coleman went to France to acquire the education necessary to become a first rate pilot, but returned to the United States in order to share that knowledge with other African Americans. Ironically, many artists found expatriation the only alternative to a fundamental dilemma. As gifted members of the race, they were called upon to aesthetically delineate a proud African American heritage, but the end product had to conform to the tastes of mainstream America. A sufficiently dazzling display of cultural excellence would, according to Locke, compel the world to admit the Negro to full American citizenship.[12] American society sought a renaissance in perspective; however, segregation constrained the artistic endeavors of some African American artists. Consequently, many of them found Europe a far more congenial setting: unsegregated if not thoroughly unprejudiced, and less likely to hold critical judgment the hostage of stereotype. Yet expatriation also constituted a brain-drain, siphoning away some of the brightest, most inspiring figures needed to form a critical mass of African American talent. Coleman seems to have been aware of the problem in deciding to return to the United States after she earned her license in France.

Finally, and most germane to this study, Coleman adapted her aviation skills to popular entertainment and inspired other African Americans to take up military and commercial aviation. In spite of her untimely death, evidence suggests that Coleman successfully persuaded other African Americans to pursue aviation as a profession, leaving a legacy for which several generations of African American pilots still honor her during an annual memorial service by flying over her graveside and dropping a wreath from the air onto it.[13]

Coleman's career also coincided with the introduction of popular culture as a serious discipline. According to M. Thomas Inge, Gilbert Seldes is credited with launching popular culture as a concept, with his publication of *The 7 Lively Arts* in 1924 in which he stated:

> That there is no opposition between the great and the lively arts. That except in a period when the major arts flourish

with exceptional vigour [sic], the lively arts are likely to be the most intelligent phenomenon of their day. That the lively arts as they exist in America today are entertaining, interesting, and important. That with a few exceptions these same arts are more interesting to the adult cultivated intelligence than most of the things which pass for art in cultured society.[14]

Since then, popular culture as a discipline, just as any other new discipline has undergone continual expansion and reassessment. The one constant, however, has been its focus primarily on white culture, to the exclusion of others.[15] Serious scholars of popular culture have provided definitions for popular culture and almost as quickly, have had to change and/or expand upon them. The nature of popular culture necessarily demands change because it is a culture simultaneously evolving with a society in transformation.

The definitions promulgated by these scholars, however, proved to be problematic at best when attempting to apply them to this study. First, because the scholars cannot arrive at a general consensus among themselves as to what constitutes "popular culture;" because integral to each is the supposition that culture is "something spiritual and transcendent," and that it can still be taught.[16] Additionally, because the majority of their investigations are dependent upon written records, African American subjects are most often neglected in these studies. Coleman, for example did not leave diaries, letters nor the like, and aviation historians have neglected her in their documented histories. Traditionally, African Americans have not maintained written records; the reasons for this are too numerous to discuss here. Perhaps Coleman's living was enough of a record of her life, and as the late Nathan I. Huggins noted, "[i]t takes a special kind of character to keep a diary, save letters, or write memoirs: one must have a sense of his own historical importance--if not to society, at least to his heirs."[17] Finally, because most paradigms of popular culture pay inadequate attention to the way a racially charged environment influences artistic production, this is the perspective of my investigation.

My application of popular culture to barnstorming is that it is a field that is derivative of the legitimate stage; it attracted large audiences from every strata of society; it appropriated its entertainment mastery from the legitimate stage; its exclusive function is to entertain. As a subject during the 1920s, aviation "as a token of American popular culture emerged in the mass media," it permeated magazines, films, advertisements and all other media traditionally associated with popular culture.[18] There is a revised definition of popular culture based on a distillation of definitions provided since 1924, in the introduction to the most recent edition of the *Handbook of American Popular Culture* (1989), accompanied by a plea from editor M. Thomas Inge, to discontinue the stratification of popular culture into high, low, mass media, popular, and the like; and instead to "describe all ... as simply culture."[19] In the same volume, Don B. Wilmeth states in the introduction to "Circus and Outdoor Entertainment," that "Of all forms of early American popular entertainment, excluding popular theater, only the outdoor amusement industry and the circus have managed to survive changing times and tastes despite noticeable alterations."[20] The stated categories under this heading are extensive, but there is no mention of flying circuses, barnstorming, aerobatics or related subjects in the ten page bibliography (193-203) provided in this section. Two examples of the resurgence of aviation barnstorming as witnessed by this author in Bloomington, Indiana and in Nairobi, Kenya in East Africa, during the latter part of the 1980s, suggest that it continues to be a popular entertainment and that it is worthy of scholarly investigation.[21]

For these reasons, and in the spirit of reassessing and expanding the perspective of popular culture, I have kept this study within the parameters of Houston Baker's paradigm, based on the premise that "[o]ne does not worship, display, or teach culture; one acknowledges it as a whole way of life grounded in history, and one necessarily lives a culture."[22] Therefore, to properly study a culture it is necessary to "pay as much attention to historical factors as one pays to technology and sociological patterns."[23] Baker's definition and suggested analytical approach exemplify my understanding of Coleman's significance to popular culture and to the African American community; as well as how to adequately disclose the interaction between both. Although Coleman's aspirations appear to be similar to those of her white counterparts, the way she pursued them was tempered by the society in which she lived.

As stated above, and discussed at length in Chapter II, Coleman's original objective was altered by the enforcement of American Jim Crow laws. While her white counterparts had to contend with sexism, these laws did not circumscribe their lives as they did Coleman's. Many white women also adopted "barnstorming" in an effort to gain entrance into the field of aviation after World War I, because they were excluded from aviation schools and from participating in commercial aviation.[24] These obstacles did not however, prevent Harriet Quimby, Matilde Moisant, Ruth Law, Katherine and Marjorie Stinson, Amelia Earhart and other white women from becoming aviatrixes who were recognized and celebrated by mainstream America. Descriptions of how these women infiltrated, and reasons for their success in the white male dominated field of aviation are explained in Chapter III.

In most instances exceptions were made for white women and some of them coalesced with white male aviators to achieve their goals. Unlike Coleman who was the lone Black woman aviator, with little support from anyone, many of these women befriended and were spiritually supportive of each other.[25] It is clear that Coleman had to endure her agonies and ecstasies without the encouragement of a women's support group. There is no mention of Coleman in Earhart's (her contemporary) memoirs for example. Coleman's awareness of white aviatrixes however, is evidenced in the memorial flight she made over the St. Charles River in Boston, in recognition of the white pioneer aviatrix Harriet Quimby (1884-1912), former drama critic, who fatally crashed there. Conversely, no records have been found of even one of Coleman's white contemporaries acknowledging her death, nor for that matter, her existence.

It is also essential to note here, that the socio-political interactions between Black and white women were adversarial during this era; rationale for these attitudes are provided in Chapter II. No discovered evidence has suggested that the relationship between Coleman and the white aviatrixes differed. Moreover, Bragg a licensed aviatrix at the time of recruitment for World War II, states that even then, "the WASP's--[Women Airforce Service Pilots]--would not let us [Blacks] into the Air Force."[26] Whereas both financial and moral support for Coleman was provided by Black males, their position in the larger society was also restricted by segregation laws and racism. In aviation, African American men and women taught each other how to fly, built airstrips together, and even shared their airplanes with each other.[27]

African American women and men worked together to achieve equality during this era, in an effort to gain entrance into mainstream America. They were unified in social and political organizations and activities that opposed the heinous crimes of racism perpetrated against Blacks collectively. Black women made a concerted effort to stamp out racism because they "... understood the relationship between the progress of the race and their own feminism;" and having experienced racism from their white sisters in temperance, suffragists and other organizations, they also understood that to achieve women's rights instead of equal rights would result in "...an empty promise if Afro-Americans were crushed under the heel of a racist power structure."[28]

Bessie Coleman was exactly what an audience primed for drama and suspense demanded. The atmosphere and activities involving African Americans defining themselves within the larger realm of American society made it possible for Coleman to define herself in that society. African Americans had long established themselves as entertainers. Since America and its socio-political and cultural institutions were in a state of transition, the late nineteenth and early twentieth centuries was an auspicious era for Coleman to expand on the popularity of the African American entertainer in an endeavor that contributed to the modification of segregation, class, and gender barriers in American society.

A NOTE ON METHODOLOGY

The methodology employed in this study is to analyze and interpret primary and secondary sources with the objective of reconstructing Coleman's life, in order to establish a rationale for her importance to the African American community specifically, and to establish her significance to the study of popular entertainment in general. Coleman's aeronautic achievements in the United States are drawn primarily from unindexed African American newspapers, the principle source of documentation of African American activities during the period under examination. Oral histories from relatives, friends, and admirers are also utilized and discussed in perspective with political, social and cultural histories of America during the latter part of the nineteenth century and into the early twentieth century. This study is presented chronologically and topically. It is important to organize major events of Coleman's life as they occurred concurrently with those of intellectual and popular histories of ideas because some of Coleman's activities were governed by both. The application of both methods provide rationale for her choice of activities and for the manner in which she pursued her objectives. And further, because after collecting, sorting, and assembling the diverse sources pertinent to reconstructing Coleman's life it became unequivocally clear to me that:

> Black American culture is characterized by a collectivistic ethos; society is not viewed as a protective arena in which the individual can work out his own destiny and gain a share of America's benefits by his own efforts. To the black American these benefits are not attained solely by individual effort, but by changes in the nature of society and the social, economic, and political advancement of a whole race of people; society, for obvious reasons, is seldom seen as a protective arena....black American culture is partially differentiated from white American culture because one of its most salient characteristics is an index of repudiation. Oral, collectivistic, and repudiative--each of these aspects helps to distinguish black American culture from white American culture.[29]

The political realm must be explored because in the United States, both state and national governments have frequently enacted and enforced segregation laws that regulate and prevent the inclusion of African Americans in democratic institutions. Subsequently, many African Americans, artists included, gradually adopted a political disposition in contending with restrictive laws. Many African

Americans acknowledged Jim Crow laws as a challenge, and found ways to circumvent the objective of these laws without actually breaking them in their pursuit for inclusion in American institutions. Initially Coleman wanted to fly because it was exciting and she knew she was capable, but when she was unsuccessful in finding a position in commercial aviation she adapted her aeronautic skills to the subfield of popular aviation. Concurrently, she developed a definite political intent to educate other African Americans in aviation to utilize it as a means to upward mobility. It is, therefore, no surprise to discover that she was in attendance at the highly political Second Pan-African Congress Paris session. This Congress was spearheaded by the renowned William Edward Burghardt DuBois whose stated purpose was to "emerge with a program of Pan-Africanism, as organized protection of the Negro world led by American Negroes."[30] Coleman's presence at this event verifies her racial and political consciousness.

The socio-political realm discussed in Chapter II is essential in determining how Coleman gained entrance and recognition into this white male-dominated field during a socially turbulent period for African Americans. The first few decades of the twentieth century were characterized by mass migrations of African Americans from the South to the North, and race riots, and lynchings in both Texas, Coleman's childhood home, and Chicago, her adopted home.[31] These events parallel the time period Coleman migrated from South to North, as well as during her eventual voyage to France.

Finally, the cultural realm is the basic foundation of any civilization, and more importantly, the foundation embraced by Bessie Coleman that immortalized her in African American communities. This study concerns itself with two American cultural institutions that were influenced by a society in transition, and in turn influenced that society. Theatre was forced to embrace more public forms of entertainment in order to appeal to the masses comprised of non-English speaking European immigrants and migrating workers from the South. African American arts and letters in many instances were forced to redefine for mass consumption after white people decided to exploit the talent of "The New Negroes."

With some minor exceptions, American Theatre as it was constituted through the nineteenth century was primarily an institution rooted in upper-class European origins, heavily influenced by, if not directly imitative of, European origins. By the early 1920s, however, several influences had converged to create a more populist theatre. As the urban centers swelled with migrants and immigrants, melodrama increased in popularity. This was a genre that promoted basic tenets of good and evil, was filled with action and suspense, and was cast with stock characters that gradually came to represent the audience. As Melodrama became more sensational it incorporated more sophisticated technology. Melodrama was eventually absorbed by film and was even more successful. Film appealed to non-English speaking immigrants and illiterate migrants, it was affordable (a nickel) to them, and its accessibility to these new urban dwellers characteristically contributed to the success of films with a highly melodramatic bent.

For African Americans this was a cultural era variously referred to as the "Harlem Renaissance," the "Black Renaissance," or the "New Negro Movement." This study will refer to the period of African American cultural recognition as the "African American cultural renaissance," and as the "New Negro Movement," because these designations reflect the renaissance's breadth in scope and location.

Bessie Coleman's shaping of aviation to didactic ends, while still managing to appeal to a large popular audience, also reflects her awareness of a massive shift in the emphases and functions of entertainment. Although there were several subgenres of melodrama, they all featured the virtuous woman as central to the melodramatic structure. Coleman consciously exploited this structure. Physically, she was petite and appeared to be frail and helpless, but in the air she became the heroine. Coleman was further aware of the emerging popularity of films and had newsreels made of her dare-devil flights in Europe which she used to promote her exhibitions in the United States. Coleman was making plans with an independent director in Florida to begin a film career when she met with untimely death.

After first compiling a list of unindexed African American newspapers that were in operation during the period under investigation, I forwarded letters of inquiry to the editors of each. Two provided names and addresses, others indicated that their files had not been preserved that far back, and many had collapsed. The newspaper still in existence and the one that most diligently covered Coleman's endeavors was *The Chicago Defender*. The microfilm collection of African American newspapers, especially *The Chicago Defender* at Indiana University proved to be indispensable to my research. With the assistance of the late Wilmer Baatz, then African American Studies Librarian at Indiana University, and with help from the Microforms librarians and the Interlibrary Loan services, I successfully acquisitioned many more African American newspapers during the five year period of my research. Their cooperation facilitated my compilation of comprehensive documentation on the life and accomplishments of Bessie Coleman.

A two part article entitled "Brave Bessie: First Black Pilot" in *Essence Magazine* May 1976, led me to Anita King, the author who graciously forwarded a brief bibliography that included two obituaries. "They Take to The Sky: Group of Midwest Women Follow Path Blazed by Pioneer Bessie Coleman," a May 1977 article in *Ebony Magazine* eventually moved me closer to Marion Coleman, Bessie

Coleman's niece. In a lengthy formal attempt to locate the author whose name did not accompany the article, I finally telephoned Janyce Givens, founder and then president of the Bessie Coleman Aviators, whose mailing address was provided in the article. I learned from these telephone conversations that Michelle Bergen, sister of actress Denise Nicholas was the author, but that she was found murdered in a rented car at LaGuardia Airport in 1979. Bergen had become an aviator and president of the Bessie Coleman Aviators during her coverage of this story. Givens further provided me with information and telephone numbers of Coleman's relatives.

Dean Stalworth, Coleman's nephew in Michigan, put me in contact with Marion Coleman, Bessie Coleman's niece and the only surviving member of the family who actually knew her aunt. She had lived with her Aunt Bessie as a youngster and continues to reside in Chicago. Stalworth made it clear that Marion is the culture-bearer of the Coleman family, very protective of their history and that it was necessary to win her confidence before I could obtain any information.[32] Several telephone conversations with Marion Coleman, during which I assured her that my interest in Coleman was strictly scholarly and not for financial profit, persuaded her to forward an autographed copy of *Bessie Coleman, Aviatrix: Pioneer of the Negro People in Aviation,* privately published by her late mother Elois Coleman Patterson in 1969. This document was indispensable to my research.[33]

It was written from Patterson's recollections, and although her dates of events are often faulty, I found her recall of events to be quite accurate. Using this small booklet as my guide, I developed a skeletal calendar. From this I began an almost daily four year journey in the Microforms department of Indiana University's Main Library where I tediously pieced together as many of the missing segments of Coleman's life as possible. I read the obituaries and worked backwards from the date of her crash. When there were indications of cities where she had performed, I read African American newspapers, if there was one in the area, and then major white newspapers for that location. I forwarded letters of inquiry to archives in Texas, Chicago, Boston, California, Langston University in Oklahoma, and the Ohio and Indiana Historical Societies. I wrote letters and had telephone conversations with records officers of hospitals where Coleman supposedly recuperated after her first airplane crash.

Many of these searches proved to be unproductive because the institutions did not respond for one reason or another, and some proved to be circuitous. For example, the response to my initial query letter in pursuit of a copy of Coleman's license to the Director General of the *Federation Aeronautique Internationale* located in France, directed me back to the National Aeronautic Association in Washington, D. C.

Preliminary inquiries to the Smithsonian Air and Space Museum were futile, but I did purchase two useful books from their Office of Government Publications--*Black Wings: The American Black in Aviation (1983), and United States Women in Aviation 1919-1929* (1983, both published by the Smithsonian Institution Press).

Marion Coleman provided me with a list of telephone numbers and addresses of family members. I forwarded postcards to all members of the family requesting telephone interviews, the dates and times left to their discretion. Most agreed, but I found during the interviews that few remembered Bessie Coleman because they were too young. I did learn however, from Lucretia V. Ware, one of Bessie's nieces, who has always lived in Texas, that the Southern relatives didn't like the "fast ways" (she enumerated--smoking, drinking, dancing) of the city assumed by the young ones after moving to Chicago. As a result of these differences the Texas Colemans did not keep in touch with the Chicago Colemans although this relative was still making payments on Bessie Coleman's Texas property.[34]

Finally, three unusual events occurred that moved my information gathering to completion. While praying for a missing trunk to materialize harboring Bessie Coleman's private letters, and/or documentation of her aeronautical ventures, Captain Richard E. Norman, Jr. donated a box of his father's, Richard E. Norman, Sr.'s films and papers to Phyllis Klotman for the Black Film Center Archives in 1985. Richard E. Norman, Sr. was a white filmmaker, entrepreneur and founder of the Norman Motion Picture Manufacturing Company, who made films featuring positive images of African Americans during the 1920s. The contents of this box included a copy of the film *The Flying Ace* (1926) in mint condition, and correspondence between Coleman and Norman. The correspondence documents that Bessie Coleman was to perform the stunt-flying in *The Flying Ace*. The melodramatic film was released in late 1926, billed as "The Greatest Airplane Mystery Story Ever Filmed."[35] Coleman's untimely death earlier that same year, however, occurred before Norman was able to shoot the planned footage of her stuntflying for the film. As a result, the "flying" scenes which appear in the film are handled by stage props parked firmly on the ground.

Also among the contents of the box was an advertisement, verifying the one-time existence of about two thousand feet of documentary film footage depicting Coleman's flights in Europe and America which were filmed by a "Pathe Camera Man." Although Coleman did not appear in *The Flying Ace,* her flights had been filmed. The possibility that I might be able to obtain this documentary footage propelled me into a renewed search. I pursued all film companies known to house documentary film footage of the 1920s. These include RKO in New York, the Sherman Grinberg Library, Inc., in Hollywood,

California, and New York, and the Thomas Cooper Library at the University of South Carolina. The latter was provided by Dr. Winona L. Fletcher who had learned that Twentieth Century-Fox Film Corporation had donated several million feet of "Movietonews" to this institution in March 1980. These inquiries were unfruitful, as each institution explained that most film from that era had chemically disintegrated in the "can" (storage containers for film).

During a luncheon discussion in 1989 with Dr. Patrick Manning, professor of history at Northeastern University, on historical events and unsung heroes of the 1920s, Manning mentioned Prince Kojo of Dahomey. Prior to this meeting, Collins and I had expended many hours in research and speculation in an attempt to discern Kojo's connection to Coleman, since he is mentioned in her biography as a close friend. He had become an enigma to us as we continued to unearth single line references to him, including some that questioned his royal authenticity, but nothing conclusive. Manning made available to me a paper compiled by him and James S. Speigler entitled "Kojo Tovalou-Houenou: Franco-Dahomean Patriot," the most comprehensvie work to date on Prince Kojo. This final piece to the Coleman puzzle compelled me to return to an investigation of Coleman's political affiliations after learning that Kojo was an authentic Prince and a commander in the Garvey Movement. The information found in this document strengthened my argument that the socio-political climate, to a large extent, defined the lives and destinies of many of the people attempting to survive during this era.

In an effort to answer the nagging question of why there appeared to be no interaction between Coleman and her white counterparts, I began to read the histories of the "club women," activists, and suffragists of the period under investigation. The works providing plausible explanations were African American, Fannie Barrier Williams', "The Club Movement Among Colored Women of America" in *A New Negro for a New Century: An Accurate and Up-To-Date Record of the Upward Struggles of the Negro Race* (1900), eds. Booker T. Washington, N. B. Wood, and Fannie Barrier. This work implies that there was customarily an adversarial relationship between African American and white women. Rosalyn Terborg-Penn verifies this implication in "Discrimination Against Afro-American Women in the Women's Movement, 1830-1920," in *The Afro-American Woman: Struggles and Images* (1978); as well as Aileen Kraditor, *The Ideas of the Women Suffrage Movement, 1899-1929* (1971); Ida B. Wells-Barnett, *Crusade for Justice: The Autobiography of Ida B. Wells-Barnett* (1970), and Mary Church Terrell's autobiography, *A Colored Woman in a White World* (1940). Since the inception of my research, several books have been published that have aided me in establishing background history on African American women in the United States, and have further strengthened my speculation as to the cause of the nonexistent relationship between Bessie Coleman and her white counterparts. The two frequently consulted in this work are Paula Giddings' now landmark study, *When and Where I Enter: The Impact of Black Women On Race and Sex in America* (1984); followed by Dorothy Sterling's *We Are Your Sisters: Black Women in the Nineteenth Century* (1984).

To determine the social, political, and cultural *milieux* of Coleman's life and times, I have relied on histories of popular entertainment, cultural histories, autobiographies, biographies, interviews, and newspaper articles. Included among popular entertainment are Robert C. Toll's *Blacking Up: The Minstrel Show in Nineteenth-Century America* (1974), *The Entertainment Machine: American Show Business in the Twentieth Century (1982), and On With the Show* (1984). Indeed, it was my reading of the latter that first peaked my interest in exploring the relationship between popular entertainment and the legitimate stage. Essential background information on African American entertainers was culled from Langston Hughes and Milton Meltzer's *Black Magic: A Pictorial History of Black Entertainers in America* (1967); Donald Bogle's *Brown Sugar: Eighty Years of America's Black Female Superstars* (1980); Henry T. Sampson's *Blacks in Blackface: A Source Book on Early Black Musical Shows* (1980); and Allen Woll's *Black Musical Theatre: From Coontown to Dreamgirls* (1989). Autobiographies and biographies have provided noteworthy details regarding the attitudes, environment, socio-political ambiance, and Black/white relationships during the period under investigation. Those frequently consulted were Langston Hughes' *The Big Sea* (1940); Robert Bolcom and William Kimball's *Reminiscing with Sissle and Blake* (1973); Stanley Dance's *The World of Earl Hines* (1977); *Crusade for Justice: The Autobiography of Ida B. Wells* (1970); and *Black Pearls: Blues Queens of the 1920s* by Daphne Duval Harrison, which is indispensable for its integration of music and biography, with an analysis of the socio-political, and cultural *milieux* that significantly altered the lives of Black women in general, and blues women in particular of the period.

Again autobiographies and biographies were utilized for their incomparable information on both Black and white aviators. Included among these are *Who Is Chauncey Spencer?* (1975) by Chauncey E. Spencer; *The Black Swallow of Death: The Incredible Story of Eugene Jacques Bullard, the World's First Black Combat Aviator* (1972) by P. J. Carisella, and James W. Ryan; *Flying Dutchman: The Life of Anthony Fokker* (1931) by Anthony H. G. Fokker, and Bruce Gould; *The Fun of It: Random Records of My Own Flying and of Women in Aviation* (1977) by Amelia Earhart; *Amelia, My Courageous Sister: Biography of Amelia Earhart, True Facts About Her Disappearance*

(1987) by Muriel Earhart Morrissey, and Carol L. Osborne; and *Lindbergh: A Biography* (1976) by Leonard Mosley.

Cultural histories employed in this study are James Weldon Johnson's *Black Manhattan* (1930); Jervis Anderson's *This Was Harlem: A Cultural Portrait: 1900-1950* (1981); David Levering-Lewis', *When Harlem Was In Vogue* (1981); Geoffrey Perrett's *America in the Twenties: A History* (1982); Allan H. Spear's *Black Chicago: The Making of A Negro Ghetto;* and Dempsey J. Travis' *An Autobiography of Black Chicago.* For a general background of African American history I have depended on John Hope Franklin's *From Slavery to Freedom: A History of Negro Americans* (1968), C. Vann Woodward's *The Strange Career of Jim Crow* (1974); and Roi Ottley's *New World A-Coming* (1943; 1968); for American History Robert Kelley's *The Shaping of the American Past* (1986). Aviation histories utilized here include *The Negro in Aviation* (1950) by Walter T. Dixon, Jr.; *Women with Wings* (1942) by Charles E. Planck; *United States Women in Aviation 1919-1929* (1983) by Kathleen Brooks-Pazmany; and *Black Wings: The American Black in Aviation* (1983) by Von Hardesty and Dominick Pisano.

Finally, detailed descriptions of flight maneuvers that appear in Chapter IV, were gleaned from *Flight Fantastic: The Illustrated History of Aerobatics* (1986) by Annette Carson; and *The Challenging Skies: The Colorful Story of Aviation's Most Exciting Years, 1919-1939* (1966) by C. R. Roseberry; and descriptions of types of airplanes were derived from *The Wonderful World of Aircraft* (1980), by John Heritage.

In determining how to organize these diverse materials, into an intelligible manuscript, I found Sandra R. Lieb's *Mother of the Blues: A Study of Ma Rainey* (1981) originally a dissertation, and Errol Hill's *Shakespeare in Sable* (1984), both useful paradigms on how to assemble fragmented pieces of information gathered from diverse sources on performers long-deceased.

IN SUMMATION: THE SIGNIFICANCE OF BESSIE COLEMAN

Errol Hill writes that,

It is clearly important that black citizens have around them reminders of those outstanding Afro-Americans who at great personal cost have striven to improve the lot of Americans, whether it be through armed struggle, political action, scientific discovery, the arts and letters, or sports and

popular entertainment. These exemplars serve as an inspiration
to present and future effort, they instill a sense of pride in
one's race, they help instruct the young about their past.
Because so much of the history of a nation is perceived
through the lives of its great men and women, the absence of
recognition seems to imply that black Americans have done
little or nothing to move this country along the road to
progress, an impression that is demonstrably untrue.[36]

There is no doubt that Bessie Coleman served "as an inspiration to
present and future effort." That she did is manifested in the present day
organization that bears her name, and in the loyalty of the African
American aviators, who still today, fly over Coleman's gravesite at
Lincoln Cemetery in Chicago, and toss a wreath onto it while airborne,
in continued recognition of "Brave Bessie."[37] Knowledge of Coleman's
efforts "instilled a sense of pride in one's race," for at least one little
girl who wrote to Coleman in 1926, "I am writing you to congratulate
you on your brave doings. I want to be an aviatrix when I get a woman.
..."[38]

Although Coleman's life was shortened because of her chosen
career, she left a contribution that the Black community still
remembers. This, then, is not solely the story of another "first," but it
belongs to a continuum that is embedded in an intangible contribution
that Coleman's legacy bequeathed to the Black community. She did not
fly trans-Atlantic flights, and her name does not grace the pages of
aviation record books. Indeed, Coleman's name is conspicuously absent
from aviation histories. This absence does not, however, diminish her
importance to the Black community, nor to popular entertainment. For
her name can be found in the pages of unindexed Afro-American
newspapers, and more importantly, on the lips of contemporary pioneer
African American aviators. Coleman did meet her stated objectives--
she became a licensed aviatrix; and she encouraged African Americans
to take up aviation as a profession.

Her decisions also affected the white community too, for she was
also a pioneer in the erosion of segregated audiences. Coleman on
several occasions refused to perform until Black spectators were
admitted into the audience with whites. Furthermore, had she not
persevered in her own aviation career, African Americans of the thirties
and thereafter, may not have persevered in pursuing aviation careers
that led to their admission into the Civilian Pilots Training Program,
and to the establishment of the Tuskeegee Airmen at Tuskeegee
Institute in Alabama where most of the African American fighter pilots
were trained for World War II.[39] All of these activities engendered
interaction between African Americans and white Americans who
legally lived in a segregated society.

It is my sincere hope that the majority of information contained herein is accurate enough to make further research on African American aviatrixes a little easier for future scholars. Hopefully, this work will not only be a meaningful contribution to the reparation of American, African American, Aviation, and Women's histories in the United States, but will also be of some service to the current reassessment of the importance of popular entertainment to American culture.

Notes

1. Joseph J. Corn, *The Winged Gospel: America's Romance with Aviation, 1900-1950* (New York: Oxford University Press, 1983) 73; Judy Lomax, "The Good Old Crazy Days in America," *Women of the Air* (New York: Dodd, Mead & Company, 1987) 33.

2. Roger E. Bilstein, "From Barnstorming to Business Flying," *Flight Patterns: Trends of Aeronautical Development in the United States, 1918-1929* (Athens: The University of Georgia Press, 1983) 62.

3. Elois Coleman Patterson, *Memoirs of the Late Bessie Coleman Aviatrix: Pioneer of the Negro People in Aviation* (Elois Patterson, 1969) N. pag.; Henry T. Sampson, *Blacks in Blackface: A Source Book on early black Musical Shows* (New Jersey: The Scarecrow Press, Inc., 1980) 21; Langston Hughes and Milton Meltzer, *Black Magic: A Pictorial History of Black Entertainers in America* (New York: Bonanza Books, 1967) 64.

4. Constance Baker Motley, "The Legal Status of the Black American," *The Black American Reference Book,* ed. Mabel M. Smythe, (New Jersey: Prentice-Hall, Inc., 1976) 102.

5. C. Van Woodward, *The Strange Career of Jim Crow*, 3rd revised edition, (New York: Oxford University Press, 1974) 117.

6. Janet Harmon Bragg, telephone interview with Elizabeth Hadley Freydberg 9 April 1988; Charles A. Lindbergh, "Aviation, Geography, and Race," *Reader's Digest* November 1939: 64-67; Enoch P. Waters, *American Diary: A Personal History of the Black Press* (Chicago: Path Press, Inc., 1987) 202; and Leonard Mosley, *Lindbergh: A Biography* (New York: Doubleday, 1976) 251.ity Press, 1974) 117.

7. Von Hardesty and Dominick Pisano, *Black Wings: The American Black in Aviation* (Washington, D.C.: National Air and Space Museum, Smithsonian Institution, 1983) 57. For continuing accounts of discrimination in the United States armed forces beyond this date see Richard M. Dalfiume, *Desegregation of the U.S. Armed Forces* (Unversity of Missouri Press, 1969); Charles C. Moskos, Jr., "Racial Integration in the Armed Forces," *The Making of Black America*, eds. August Meier and Elliot Rudwick, vol. 2 (New York: Atheneum Press, 1969); "U.S. Armed Forces: 1950; Record of Negro Integration in the Services Since President Truman's Executive Order," *Our World,* June 1951, 11-35; Wallace Terry, "Black Soldiers and Vietnam," *The Black American: A Documentary History*, ed. Leslie H. Fishel, Jr., and Benjamin Quarles (New York: William Morrow and Co., 1970); "Armed Services Integration," *Crisis*, July 1950: 443; "How Integration Has Worked in the Arm [sic] Forces," *Sepia,* December 1959, 14-17;

MacGregor, Morris J. Jr., and *Integration of the Armed Forces 1940-1965* (Washington, D.C.: U. S. Government Printing Office, 1980).

8. Bragg, telephone interview 9 April 1988; Phillip Hart telephone interview with Elizabeth Hadley Freydberg, 21 May 1988.

9. Alain Locke, "The New Negro," *The New Negro,* ed. Alain Locke (New York: Atheneum, 1980) 5.

10. My interpretation of Carl Van Vechten's novel, *Nigger Heaven* (New York: 1926), in which he exaggerates and provides a guide to the "seedy" environments of Black night-life in Harlem for the pleasure of white people. The title itself was then and still is controversial since it is derived from the place to which Blacks were remanded in the theatre during the Jim Crow era. Although Nancy Cunard's *Negro* (New York: 1934), is a compendium of writings by several people, she too accentuates the sleazy elements of Harlem. Also see, William Burghardt DuBois, for a discussion on the controversial aspects of Van Vechten's novel in "DuBois' Review of *Nigger Heaven,*" *The Crisis* (1926), *The New Negro Renaissance: An Anthology* (New York: Holt, Rinehart and Winston, 1975) 193-194.

11. Richard Bardolph, *The Negro Vanguard,* (Connecticut: Negro Universities Press, 1959) 214.

12. Locke 15-16.

13. Janet Harmon Waterford (Bragg), "Race Interest In Aviation In Actuality Begins With Advent of Bessie Coleman," *Chicago Defender,* 28 March, 1936: 1; "Granted Pilots License [Dorothy Darby: Parachute Jumper]" *Chicago Defender,* 21 May 1938: 1; Harold Hurd, telephone conversation with Elizabeth Hadley Freydberg upon his return from the event 2 May 1989.

14. M. Thomas Inge, *Handbook of American Popular Cuture, Second Edition, Revised and Enlarged,* ed. Thomas Inge (New York: Greenwood Press, 1989) xxi; Gilbert Seldes, *The Seven Lively Arts,* (1924; New York: Harper and Brothers, 1957) 294-295.

15. Houston A. Baker, Jr., "Completely Well: One View of Black American Culture," *Key Issues in the Afro-American Experience,* eds. Nathan I. Huggins, Martin Kilson, and Daniel M. Fox, vol. 1 (New York: Harcourt Brace Jovanovich, Inc., 1971) 20; Lawrence W. Levine, preface, *Black Culture and Black Consciousness: Afro-American Folk Thought from Slavery and Freedom* (New York: Oxford University Press, 1977) x. See also Inge, introduction, xxi-xxxiii. Inge describes the evolution of the study of popular culture and lists the landmark works in this field. Included in this list are Henry Nash Smith, *Virgin Land* (1950); Dwight MacDonald, *Against the American Grain* (1962); Russel B. Nye's *The Unembarrassed Muse* (1971) and John Cawalti, *The Six-Gun Mystique* (1971). This author studied all of the above listed books, in addition to autobiographies of *Andrew Jackson, and*

Benjamin Franklin, the novels of *Horatio Algers* and other white men; as required texts in two American Studies core seminars on popular culture at Indiana University/Bloomington, taught by then chairperson, Dr. Steven Stein in 1982.

16. Baker, Jr., 20. Although Baker specifically cites Raymond Williams, *Culture and Society, 1780-1950* (New York: Columbia University Press, 1958), we can include Inge, who continues an attempt to define popular culture in the new enlarged, revised edition of the *Handbook of American Popular Cuture*, introduction, xxiv-xxvi; Ray B. Browne, "Popular Culture: Notes Toward a Definition," *Popular Culture and the Expanding Consciousness*, ed. Ray B. Browne (New York: John Wiley & Sons, Inc., 1973); and C. W. E. Bigsby, ed., *Approaches to Popular Culture* (London: Edward Arnold, 1976) in which appears seven "possible approaches to popular culture," 3-149.

17. Nathan I. Huggins, "Afro-American History: Myths, Heroes, Reality," *Key Issues in the Afro-American Experience*, vol. 1, 6.

18. Bilstein, "Symbolism and Imagery," *Flight Patterns*, 150-153.

19. Inge xxxi. Inge has refined his definition from those of Ray B. Browne, C. W. E. Bigsby, Michael J. Bell, Norman F. Cantor and Michael S. Werthman, xiv-xxxi.

20. Don B. Wilmeth, "Circus and Outdoor Entertainment," *Handbook of Popular Culture*, 173.

21. Hoosier Airshow '89, Monroe County Airport, Bloomington, Indiana, 10 September 1989; "Green Eagles" of the Kenyan Army, 1989 Nairobi International Show, Nairobi, Kenya, East Africa, 30 September 1989.

22. Baker, Jr., 20-21.

23. Baker, Jr., 20.

24. Lomax 34.

25. Lomax, "Amelia Earhart: America's Winged Legend," 77.

26. Bragg, telephone interview 9 April 1988. Bragg, a nurse and pilot continued to relate a story of how she went to a recruitment center in Chicago to sign up for service during World War II. When she displayed her pilot's license the woman recruiting officer visibly flustered, packed up her briefcase and rapidly departed saying that she had to check with headquarters to find out if she would be breaking rules even if she were to interview Bragg.

27. Bragg, telephone interview 9 April 1988.

28. Paula Giddings, *When and Where I Enter: The Impact of Black Women on Race and Sex in America* (New York: William Morrow and Company, Inc., 1984) 126-128. For more comprehensive discussions on the adversarial relationships between African American and white women suffragists, see Giddings "To Choose Again Freely," Chapter III; and "The Quest for Woman Suffrage (Before World War I),"

Chapter VII; Rosalyn Terborg-Penn, "Discrimination Against Afro-American Women in the Women's Movement, 1830-1920," *The Afro-American Woman: Struggles and Images,* eds. Sharon Harley and Rosalyn Terborg-Penn (New York: Kennikat Press, 1978); and Aileen Kraditor, *The Ideas of the Women Suffrage Movement, 1899-1929* (New York: Anchor Books/Doubleday, 1971). Beah Richards succinctly crystalizes a history of various degrees of antagonism between white and Black women in her one woman play "A Black Women Speaks" (1950), *9 Plays by Black Women,* ed. Margaret B. Wilkerson (New York: New American Library, 1986) 33-39.

29. Baker, Jr., 32.

30. W.E.B. DuBois, *The Autobiography of W.E.B. Du Bois: A Soliloquy on Viewing My Life from the Last Decade of Its First Century* (New York: International Publishers, 1968) 289; *The Crisis: A Record of the Darker Races,* 25:1 (November, 1922) 75-76.

31. See Carl Sandburg, *The Chicago Race Riots: July, 1919,* preface by Ralph McGill, intro. Walter Lippmann (1919, 1947, New York: Harcourt, Brace & World, Inc., 1969). There are three plays written by African American playwrights that depict the hostile racial environment of Chicago. Theodore Ward's *Big White Fog* (1938), Richard Wright's *Native Son* (1941), and Lorraine Hansberry's *A Raisin in the Sun* (1959). Ward addresses the diverse political ideologies (Garveyism, Communism and Capitalism) that were prevalent among African Americans during the 1920s. Whereas Wright focuses on the inequities of housing, employment, and education for African Americans, Hansberry directs attention to "racially restrictive convenants" employed to exclude African Americans from residing in white neighborhoods.

32. Dean Stallworth, telephone interview with Elizabeth Hadley Freydberg 24 October 1984.

33. During my interviews in Chicago January 1985, I received another copy from David Biencke's son (see Chapter IV).

34. Lucretia V. Ware, telephone interview with Elizabeth Hadley Freydberg 7 November 1984.

35. *The Flying Ace* promotional materials. Courtesy of the Black Film Center/Archives. Professor Phyllis R. Klotman, Director. Indiana University, Bloomington.

36. Errol Hill, *Black Heroes: Seven Plays,* (New York: Applause Theatre Book Publishers, 1989) viii.

37. Rufus A. Hunt, "Bessie Coleman--The World's First Black Female Pilot;" "Salute to a Nervy Lady [Bessie Coleman]," *Chicago Tribune* 8 May 1980: N. pag.

38. Letter from Ruby Mae McDuffie to Bessie Coleman. Appears in Evangeline Roberts, "Chicago Pays Parting Tribute to 'Brave Bessie'

Coleman," *Chicago Defender*, May 15, 1926: 2. The letter is dated at "Jacksonville, Fla, 29th April, 1926."

39. Von Hardesty and Dominick Pisano, *Black Wings: The American Black in Aviation,* (Washington, D. C.: National Air and Space Museum, 1983) 19.

II

Present Possibilities and Future Forces:
A Socio-Political Overview

The Negro race is the only race without aviators and I want to interest the Negro in flying and thus help in the best way I'm equipped to uplift the colored race.

Bessie Coleman[1]

In order to place Coleman in the proper context of popular entertainment, it is necessary to provide a brief overview of the political, social, and cultural *milieux* of the late nineteenth and early twentieth centuries, since some of these events tempered her decisions and redirected the course of her life. Several political, social, and cultural events paradoxically influenced the lives of African Americans and women and the field of entertainment in the United States between 1896, the year of Coleman's birth, and 1926, the year of her death. Although political, social and cultural histories are often studied separately by academicians, it is necessary to trace their interaction in order to understand both Coleman's motivations and her contributions.

During the latter part of the nineteenth century and the first quarter of the twentieth century the United States was undergoing a turbulent social metamorphosis precipitated by the industrial revolution, slave emancipation, immigration and World War I. American political, social and cultural institutions were affected by this transition. Politically there was a rise of both white supremacy and Black Nationalism. Socially there was both segregation of, and interaction between the races. Culturally there was a divergence of high culture for the elite and popular culture for the masses. The lines between the two became more ambiguous as the different classes, races and sexes began to interact in the public realm. The political became embroiled with the cultural. The Emancipation Proclamation (1863), the initiation of federal Segregation Laws (1896), the United States' entrance into World War I (1917),

Women's suffrage (1920), and Permanent Immigration Restriction Laws (1924) designed to augment the white populace, and restrict an increase of the colored populace in American urban centers, are all political activities that eventually transformed the social structure, spawned interaction between diverse elements of society and gave rise to new cultural movements. Although African Americans began their migration from South to North and West in 1865 in search of jobs and better living conditions, the greatest number migrated between 1870 and 1921.

During Reconstruction, African Americans had attempted to improve their condition by working and building their homes in the South. Their ambitions were riddled with obstacles however, when in 1877, the Hayes administration terminated Reconstruction with the removal of federal troops that had been stationed in the South at the end of the Civil war to enforce the laws of Reconstruction. Almost immediately after the troops vacated the South, vigilante groups embarked upon a crusade of intimidation tactics designed to keep African Americans in their pre-Civil War subservient positions. Such tactics included whippings, lynchings, burning down African American communities, and the implementation of Black Codes (state laws that defined and regulated issues concerning vagrancy, work contracts, employment, and roles in court proceedings) and convict-lease laws.[2] The "separate but equal" doctrine was put into effect by the Supreme Court in the case of *Plessy v. Ferguson* in 1896, the year of Coleman's birth; it was not entirely overturned until 1954 in the case of *Brown v. Board of Education of Topeka*. These combined events fostered the African American migration to Northern urban centers during the latter part of the Nineteenth Century.

As some whites escalated their brutal harassment tactics against African Americans, three dominant philosophies predicated on African American self-help and racial pride emerged. Booker T. Washington (1856-1915), William Edward Burghardt Du Bois (1868-1963), and Marcus Garvey (1887-1940) are credited with successfully articulating these philosophies between the late 1890s and early 1920s. Washington emphasized industrial and vocational education for African Americans, while Du Bois stressed the importance of African Americans attaining a liberal arts education. Garvey emphasized Black Nationalism, asserting that African Americans had to establish their own economic and political base separate from and independent of white people. All believed education to be the panacea for upward mobility of African Americans, but the emphasis in each program differed.

Washington built Tuskegee Institute (1881), an Agriculture and Mechanical (A & M) institution to educate African Americans vocationally. He died in 1915, however, without witnessing the brutal backlash meted out to African Americans by white vigilante groups resentful of African Americans who had achieved middle-class status in the South through attaining an industrial and vocational education, hard work and perseverance. In many instances, instead of garnering the respect of whites, knowledge of prosperous African Americans unleashed deep-seated resentment and hostility among some white Southerners.[3] Subsequently, many successful African Americans were compelled to leave the South. African Americans who migrated North, were herded together with other groups streaming into the cities, as economic competition for bottom-rung jobs displaced white American males from menial positions.

Furthermore, while African Americans were migrating to Northern urban centers, immigrants from central, eastern and southern Europe were also settling in Northern cities in search of work and opportunities for a better life. Now the composition of the factory workers consisted of African American men and women, white American women, and immigrants of both genders. This mixture of ethnic groups not only exacerbated tense, crowded living conditions, but it strained race and working relations as well.[4] White factory owners and native factory workers favored the European workers because they were Caucasian. Thus one of the many manifestations of racism in the factories was in the relegation of African Americans to menial labor and positions objectionable to white workers. United States cities were fraught with workers' strikes and race riots at the turn of the century. During these strikes African Americans in search of work were often used as "strikebreakers."[5]

At the end of World War I, the backlash increased and ignited into brutal race riots. White supremacists believed that African Americans, who had fought a war on foreign soil where they were treated as equals, would return home and expect to be treated in the same manner; they wanted to prevent this from occurring. African American soldiers were indeed disillusioned when they returned home from "the war to end all wars," only to discover that their war for equality in the United States had just begun. African Americans were fired from jobs they had acquired during the war, so that returning white soldiers could regain their former employment, while returning African American soldiers were simply not hired.

Social organizations such as the National Association for the Advancement of Colored People (1909) and The National Urban League (1910), initially established to assist African American migrants in locating employment and in adjusting to their Northern lifestyles, began to expand their focus beyond these objectives to include political issues and to develop legal strategies to combat lynching and race riots. The N.A.A.C.P. embarked upon a campaign to force the Federal government to pass anti-lynch laws to protect African Americans. At the same time as the development of these organizations there arose a proliferation of "Race" novels and dramatic works that presented themes of upward mobility.[6] There developed among many African Americans a desire to be seen as merely the blackest American. These issues may have been social, but they were born out of a politically hostile environment with the implementation of federal Segregation Laws that restricted daily activities of African Americans nationwide during the Woodrow Wilson Administration (1912-1920).

As segregation laws further curtailed their entrance into mainstream America, African American people in the United States began to seek alternative means to achieve first-class citizenship, maintain some semblance of their self-respect, and to achieve economic and political stability that would enable them to provide for their families. Disillusioned African American masses in large numbers began to turn away from an integrationist philosophy and embrace separatism through enlistment in the Black Nationalist movement led by Marcus Garvey. Many of the lower and working classes believed his Universal Negro Improvement Association (UNIA) would provide them the opportunities for upward mobility. In terms of sheer numbers it was the most successful movement of the era because Garvey appealed to all Blacks irrespective of origin, education, or profession, although the majority of the membership was comprised of lower and working classes. Consequently the membership roster of the UNIA reflected a constituency that included for example, Emmett J. Scott (1873-1957), one time private secretary to Booker T. Washington and Howard University's registrar; and Henrietta Vinton Davis (1860-1941), "a superb elocutionists and internationally renowned interpreter of Shakespearean heroines."[7] Scott was knighted by Washington, and Davis was a member for at least twelve years and served as national and international organizer and as director and vice president of the Black Star Line. Garvey, an admirer of Booker T. Washington's accomplishments as a business man, had corresponded with him and was encouraged by Washington to come to the United States, but Washington died before Garvey arrived in Harlem, in 1916. Garvey immediately engaged himself in organizing branches of the UNIA in northern cities with the largest concentration of African Americans such as Detroit, Philadelphia, Pittsburgh, Cleveland, and Cincinnati.

He rallied African Americans in both Chicago and New York where he established the two largest branches of the UNIA, with headquarters located in Harlem. Garvey's Black Nationalist philosophy embodied tenets similar to those of the N.A.A.C.P. and the National Urban League regarding race pride, and racial uplift through education and self-help. Whereas the other organizations were integrationist in their perspectives, however, Garvey advocated separatism. He believed that in order for Black people to achieve equity in mainstream America they would have to divorce themselves from political and financial dependence on white America.[8] Garvey argued that belief in Black inferiority permeated the very fabric of mainstream America, functioning to keep Black people psychologically debilitated as they began to believe in their own inferiority. He therefore advocated the establishment of separate Black institutions that would promote racial pride among Black people, and initiate financial and political stability in the Black community. To enhance the self-esteem of the people, notwithstanding his love of pageantry, Garvey launched auxiliaries of the UNIA that included nurses, motor and flying corps, and a shipping line. He established the Empire of Africa for which he served as president and appointed others giving them ranks of nobility such as Potentates, knights, and dukes. All wore elaborate uniforms and displayed much "pomp and circumstance" at conferences, conventions and in parades.[9]

In an effort to attain financial stability for Black communities, Garvey's business endeavors included the founding of the Negro Factories Corporation that operated a consortium of grocery stores, a publishing house, a restaurant and several other Black run businesses including the Black Star Line responsible for transporting merchandise between the United States and the West Indies and Black people who wanted to move to Africa. The Black Star Line was indispensable to Garvey's very popular Back-to-Africa movement, that encouraged the return of Black people to the Motherland. Garvey built a Liberty Hall in each city that had a branch of the UNIA. These halls, were community centers for social and cultural events. In addition they housed a court making it possible for Blacks to circumvent white courts for the resolution of domestic arguments, the performance of weddings and funerals, and to obtain passports for Back-to-Africa travel.[10]

By the turn of the century a group of educated African Americans emerged as leaders of their communities in both New York and Chicago--the same hotbeds of activity where Bessie Coleman began her aviation career. Coleman, dated Prince Kojo Touvalou-Houénou, of Dahomey, Africa who was also a Potentate in Garvey's U.N.I.A., and she attended the 1921 Second Pan African Congress organized by W.E.B. Du Bois. They were the "New Negro," the "New Black bourgeoisie," and "Race" men and women. All of these titles alluded to those who emphasized racial uplift, and to those who understood that whatever endeavor they undertook as individuals, the consequences would be reflective of the entire race. Du Bois referred to this group as "The Talented Tenth." His rationale for the existence of this group was derived from his belief that ten percent of any race or group of people will be intellectually gifted, and African Americans were no exception. They were active in the political, social and cultural realms of American communities. They were the founders and members of the N.A.A.C.P. and the National Urban League. Both of these organizations were interracial and of mixed gender, in spite of *defacto* and *dejure* discriminatory practices in the United States. They discussed racial solidarity and economic and political equity for their people vociferously and eloquently in their organizations' literary organs, *Crisis* (1910), and *Opportunity* (1923). Elliott Rudwick writes of this evolving African American intelligentsia that:

> Between the years 1910 and 1920, the race experienced an increase in literacy, and, in addition, more Negroes than ever before were attending colleges. Consequently, leaders and followers were ready to assert their rights, and the Negro press influenced and reflected this determination. The growth of the N.A.A.C.P. itself exemplified the new fervor of the race. For instance, by 1919, the organization claimed 91,203 members, which was more than twice the number it had the year before.[11]

In addition to publishing political articles throughout the 1920s, *Crisis* and *Opportunity* also published the works of budding young African American artists, thus providing a forum that brought their works to the attention of the white *nouveau riche*. White philanthropists later became eager to finance and encourage African Americans to produce quintessential African American cultural works. Burgeoning industrialization had created opportunities for previously poor segments of the American social and economic structure to stockpile large amounts of money within a single lifespan. The offspring of this conspicuously wealthy new class, however, had not yet acquired an appreciation of staid and traditional outlets for their wealth. To phrase it another way, they had not been educated in European classicism and tradition, and became dreadfully bored. Patronage to deserving Negro artists was a means of disposing of excess wealth in return for novelty and amusement, as well as a way for youngsters to assuage the mild pricking of social conscience.

The phenomenon of patronage spurred the phenomenon now known as the Harlem Renaissance, one of the most vigorous cultural and artistic movements during the decade of the 1920s. At the same time, however, patrons George Foster Peabody and others earned themselves derisive nicknames like Zora Neale Hurston's sneering term "Negrotarians."[12] An unprecedented number of African Americans were given money to produce art authentically representative of their own culture. However, it was still the white patrons, exercising their prerogative to withhold payment, who dictated what was authentic and what was not; an artist who did not follow his or her patron's sense of what constituted authentic African American cultural expression was liable to be summarily cut from the payroll.[13] This Renaissance spawned the development of African American arts, however, because even though white people did not yet know what was *authentic* African American art they financially backed Black artists to define what that art was. Nevertheless, Alain Locke captures the optimistic ethos of the 1920s as an era when he suggests that at the same time white America was attempting to develop arts and letters that reflected an authentic national American art, so too were African Americans.[14]

This was the "Jazz Age," so anointed by F. Scott Fitzgerald who described the youth of the 1920s as "a new generation grown up to find all Gods dead, all wars fought, all faiths in man shaken."[15] This disillusionment was mirrored in the behavior of American youth, both Black and white, although their reasons for dissatisfaction with the society in which they lived diverged. The "Roaring Twenties," or the "Jazz Age," was born for and out of this generation. With more leisure time, the youngsters were restless. The social mores and entertainments that amused their parents had become boring and monotonous to these people. The young of all classes began to seek more exciting entertainment; the rich had an excess of leisure time, and the poor were in search of an outlet from the drudgery of their daily work. The twenties was further distinguished by its hotels, cabarets, speakeasies, and dance halls, all developed as playgrounds for the children of the wealthy.

The interaction between the "New Negroes," and the "lost generation" formed the nucleus of a potential new class in society. Both the "lost generation," and the "New Negro" were responsible for engendering new forms of entertainment. The "lost generation" sought these new forms in African American neighborhoods after dark, and the "New Negroes" a "found generation" provided them with new forms of entertainment in music, theatre, and literature. The "Jazz Age" was borne out of this affiliation. These two groups interacted irrespective of the segregation laws. It was a time when the "New Negroes" asserted themselves as proud African Americans. Langston Hughes, a prolific literary figure of the period, exemplifies that assertion in his declaration that,

> We younger Negro artists who create now intend to express our individual dark-skinned selves without fear or shame. If white people are pleased we are glad. If they are not, it doesn't matter. We know we are beautiful. And ugly too. The tom-tom cries and the tom-tom laughs. If colored people are pleased we are glad. If they are not, their displeasure doesn't matter either. We build our temples for tomorrow, strong as we know how, and we stand on top of the mountain, free within ourselves.[16]

The crowded city is an element parallel in significance to that of bored people. The Black migrants and the European immigrants both made their homes in the urban centers of New York and Chicago because that is where they found work. These groups, forced to live together in close quarters initially because of economics, fostered an intercultural synthesis and exchange that subsequently engendered a new society.

African American artists contributed more works to the body of American arts and letters during the "New Negro Movement" than ever before. Many scholars have focused on this "Renaissance" as primarily literary and confined to Harlem. In actuality, it was a cultural movement that materialized in African American communities nationwide. While it is true that a core of African American intelligentsia lived in New York, the African American cultural awakening was manifested in all arts and letters, and occurred throughout the country. African American cultural organizations flourished nationwide. All promoted race-pride and cultural self-awareness. Harlem drew attention because it had become one of the two largest African American communities in the country. It was the cultural center of the United States and housed the major theatres, publishing houses, banks, and white philanthropists.

African American artists, both women and men, were not confined to one genre, but created in several. Zora Neale Hurston and James Weldon Johnson, for example, created music, literary works, and dramatic works; while Langston Hughes wrote poetry in African American blues and jazz music forms, fiction, non-fiction and dramatic works. Eubie Blake, Noble Sissle, Aubrey Lyles, and Flournoy Miller redefined the roles of African Americans for Broadway, and devised the format that was adopted into American musical theatre with their musical *Shuffle Along* (1921). In addition to launching the careers of many African American stars in show business--Josephine Baker, Ethel Waters, and Florence Mills, to name a few--*Shuffle Along* included a tender love scene (a sentiment white people considered alien to African Americans), and "blended story and music into an organic whole in a manner which did not become common in American musical comedies until the late 1940s."[17] This was also the musical that Langston Hughes lauded as the catalyst that provided the "proper push--a pre-Charleston kick--to that Negro vogue of the 20's, that spread to books, African sculpture, music, and dancing," now referred to as the Harlem Renaissance.[18] Because *Shuffle Along* made Broadway moguls realize that there was a profit to be made from Black subjects beyond minstrel shows, it secured invitations for African American musicals to perform on the Great White Way for at least a decade thereafter.[19]

WOMEN AS POLITICAL AND CULTURAL ACTIVISTS

As stated earlier, the shortage of workers precipitated by World War I was responsible for women leaving hearth and home to enter the labor force. Although white middle-class women had begun to work outside of the home as they became more educated, this war thrust a diverse group of women into the public realm, a realm that was previously inhabited and dominated solely by men. The more visibility women achieved in the business world, the more they demanded to be accorded visibility in the political world of American life. African American women had, however, always been in the labor force since their days of enslavement. Consequently they were now expected by fathers and husbands to lead a more genteel existence. But after emancipation many African American women remained instead in the public realm where they worked harmoniously with African American men toward the achievement of racial and political equity, and also established organizations for their own social, political and cultural improvement. The women at the forefront of establishing these organizations were known as "club women." Contrary to the suggestion of this title, these women were not organized to advance their positions as social butterflies, but emerged as activists, artists, and suffragists who expressed that among their primary concerns was

> How to help and protect some defenseless and tempted young women; how to aid some poor boy to complete a much-coveted education; how to lengthen the short school term in some impoverished school district; how to instruct and interest deficient mothers in the difficulties of child training ...[20]

After frequent skirmishes with white women, rejection from white women clubs, and repeated scurrilous verbal, written, and physical attacks against African American women, the colored club women emerged nationally in 1896 when they established the National Association of Colored Women (NACW); an amalgamation of local African American women's clubs from throughout the nation.[21] This self-help organization functioned as an assertive, positive inspirational force for the upward mobility and recognition of Black women in the United States. Fannie Barrier Williams delineates the contrast between the goals and objectives of these clubs and those of their white counterparts:

> The club movement among colored women reaches into the sub-social condition of the entire race. Among white women

clubs mean the forward movement of the best women in the
interest of the best womanhood. Among colored women the
club is only one of many means for the social uplift of a race.
Among white women the club is the onward movement of the
already uplifted.[22]

The colored club women recognized themselves as "the real new
woman in American life," and were, just as their male counterparts,
members of the educated, race conscious, African American elite.[23]
Three of the more influential "club women" of the decade were political
and cultural activists Ida B. Wells-Barnett (1862-1931) who
corresponded with Bessie Coleman and eulogized her at the Chicago
Funeral, Mary Church Terrell (1863-1954), and Mary Burnett Talbert
(1866-1923). Wells-Barnett and Terrell were also founding members of
the N.A.A.C.P. in 1909, while Talbert served as vice-president and
director.[24] In addition to meeting their responsibilities to that
organization, they established local organizations in their individual
communities.

Ida B. Wells-Barnett, teacher, newspaper editor, suffragist, and
activist, originally from Tennessee, adopted Chicago as her home in
1893. As a newspaper columnist for the *Age,* the *Detroit Plain Dealer,*
the *Indianapolis Freeman,* the *Gate City Press* and the *Little Rock Sun,*
and as editor of her own *Chicago Weekly* and *The Conservator* (1805-
1909) Wells-Barnett wrote and printed scathing articles lamenting the
maltreatment of African American women, and exposés on lynching and
discrimination in American society. She occasionally called African
American male leaders to task for not taking an aggressive stance
toward the resolution of these inequities. After a childhood friend,
Thomas Moss was lynched, Wells-Barnett became an outstanding orator
who lectured throughout the United States and England educating people
about the bestial practice of lynching and discrimination in the United
States.[25] Although her life was threatened on numerous occasions, her
printing press and editorial offices of the Memphis *Free Speech* were
destroyed, and she fled Tennessee hotly pursued by a lynch mob, Wells-
Barnett continued her crusade against lynching with two pistols in her
skirt pockets for protection.[26] She compiled her research of hundreds of
lynching cases into a work entitled *A Red Record: Tabulated Statistics
and Alleged Causes of Lynchings in the United States, 1892-1893-
1894,* the first statistical records amassed on lynching in the United
States. Her research revealed that the majority of the lynchings were not
perpetrated because African American males violated virtuous white
women, as white people had maintained.[27] Rather, they were perpetrated
by malicious white men who believed in the inferiority of African
Americans, and who resented their financial and educational
achievements.

Wells-Barnett, not one to engage in idle destructive criticism of functioning organizations, initiated her own organizations when she believed that others were not meeting the needs of African Americans. In addition to being one of the founding members of the National Association for the Advancement of Colored People (N.A.A.C.P.), she helped found the National Association of Colored Women (NACW) in 1896, the year of Coleman's birth; she also used her own salary as municipal court probation officer to establish and finance the Negro Fellowship League (1908), a shelter, recreation and employment center for southern migrants. She responded not only to racism, but to sexism within the feminist ranks as well. Wells-Barnett organized the Alpha Suffrage Club (1913) for African American women in response to the dissension created by white suffragists who were afraid that African Americans would receive the right to vote before them.[28] In an attempt to discredit African American women, some white women published deleterious statements casting suspicion on the moral character of African American women.[29] Wells-Barnett defiantly marched in the suffrage parade in Washington, D.C. in 1913, after she was told by the white National American Women's Suffrage Association (NAWSA) that she and the Alpha Suffrage Club "could not march with the all-White Chicago contingent of suffragists for fear of offending southern white women."[30]

Wells-Barnett, who was living in Chicago during the notorious race-riot of 1919, traveled throughout the United States during the height of race riots between 1918 and 1927 to investigate and gain first-hand knowledge as to the causes of the riots. Hers was the second lawsuit initiated against a public transportation facility (Sojurner Truth initiated the first) in the case of *Wells vs. Chesapeake, Ohio & Southwestern Railroad* (1884) for segregation practices; she won temporarily.[31]

Wells-Barnett also contributed time and finances to the theatre. As a young woman she had aspirations of becoming an actress and even studied elocution and gave recitations of "Lady Macbeth's sleepwalking scene at local concerts."[32] Dorothy Sterling indicates that Wells-Barnett loved theatre so much that whenever she had the chance to attend the theatre she recorded the event in her diary. She wrote in her diary for example, after having seen Edwin Booth in performance in *Hamlet* and *Othello*, that he was "the greatest living actor;" that she found *The Mikado* "bright and sparkling, with no suggestion of the coarse of vulgar;" and that she enjoyed *The Count of Monte Cristo* and *The Burning of Moscow*.[33] Ida B. Wells-Barnett used her political influence in later years to organize one hundred affluent African American women to raise money for the operation of the Pekin Theatre in Chicago, much to the displeasure of the pastors of Bethel A. M. E. and Olivet (prominent African American Baptist churches in Chicago). This was the first legitimate African American theatre in the United States (1904).[34] It provided a much needed venue for artists Will Marion Cook, Abbie Mitchell, Charles Gilpin, Flournoy Miller, Aubrey Lyles, Bob Cole, George Walker, Bert Williams and many others. Mary Church Terrell, a political activist and initially a friend of Wells-Barnett, was one who knew too well the experience of being judged by her gender and race in the United States rather than her intellect. She like Coleman later, went to Europe where she could develop her intellect free of these prejudicial barriers.

Mary Church Terrell was a suffragist, lecturer, activist and an Oberlin College graduate whose wealthy father forbade her to teach because he considered such an occupation beneath her. Terrell's home and base of activism was primarily in Washington, D. C. where in 1892, she became the first African American woman appointed to the District Board of Education, a post she held for seven years.[35] To instill African American children with pride in their heritage she established Frederick Douglas Day making Washington schools the first in the nation to celebrate an African American.[36] Terrell was instrumental in founding the National Association of Colored Women in 1896 along with Ida B. Wells Barnett, and was elected president of this Association in 1897. She lectured from Wellesley to Fisk on the status of women of color in the United States. In addition to meeting the opposition of white suffragists, Terrell a woman of high academic achievements, forced white women in the Academy to extend membership to women of color in the American Association of University Women (AAUW) and after a three year struggle, became the first African American woman to be admitted in 1949.[37] Among her many accomplishments she was a charter member of the National Association of College Women (1924), President of the Coordination Committee for the Enforcement of Anti-Discrimination Laws for the District of Columbia, and a delegate to the International Congress of Women in Berlin where she lectured in French and German in 1904.[38] Through lectures and demonstrations, Terrell vigorously fought for the passage of the Nineteenth Amendment, that granted women the right to vote. Barnett's childhood friend Thomas Moss was also Terrell's childhood friend. Terrell also, became actively involved in crusades against lynching for more than thirty years after he was lynched. Included among her anti-lynching activities was a meeting she and Frederick Douglass had with President Benjamin Harrison during which they requested that Harrison condemn lynching during his annual address to Congress by proposing anti-lynching legislation; the President did not oblige them.[39] Terrell addressed diverse audiences, including segregated ones, in order to persuade them to join the fight against racial injustices perpetrated against African Americans. In 1953, Mary Church Terrell could still be found marching in a demonstration in Washington, D.C. in an effort to purge the nation's capital of segregated public facilities.

Mary Burnett Talbert, also an Oberlin College graduate, with a Ph.D. from the University of Buffalo, served her country by selling thousands of dollars worth of United States Liberty Bonds, and served in France as a Red Cross nurse during World War I. After the war she returned home and actively joined in the fight for racial and political equity in the United States. Talbert simultaneously served as vice-president and director of the National Association for the Advancement of Colored People and president of the National Federation of Women's clubs (1916-1920). As chairperson of the Anti-Lynching Committee, she campaigned throughout the United States for passage of the Dyer Anti-Lynching Bill, and organized other African American women to campaign against the construction of a "Mammy Monument" in Washington, D.C.[40] In 1920, she was a delegate to the International Council of Women in Christiania, Norway. She continued to travel and lecture on race relations and women's rights throughout Europe.[41] Mary Burnett Talbert served as president of the Frederick Douglass Memorial Association, and was responsible, along with others for the restoration of the Frederick Douglass Home at Anacostia in 1922.[42]

African American women were also in the vanguard of the cultural renaissance nationwide. Sarah Breedlove (1867-1919) was born in Louisiana, the daughter of former slaves, orphaned at five, married to C. J. Walker at fourteen, a mother and widow at twenty. After the death of her husband, Walker washed clothes for wealthy white people to support herself and her daughter.[43] Determined not to be a washerwoman for the rest of her life, and distressed over balding, she took "two dollars and a dream" in 1905 and established what was to become the most successful "hair culturist" and cosmetics enterprise catering primarily to Black women. Through innovative marketing skills including advertisements in African American periodicals (The *Chicago Defender* among them), Madame C. J. Walker amassed a formidable mail-order list of customers nationwide that was instrumental in her expeditiously becoming "a millionaire--one of the first women, white or black, to achieve this goal by her own efforts in business."[44]

By the time she had become a personal friend of Garvey's, and a "club woman," Walker had already embodied the ideals of the UNIA and the club women--racial uplift through education and Black economic support.[45] After door-to-door marketing of her products in cities throughout the country, she finally in 1910, chose Indianapolis, Indiana as the location for her beautician school and the permanent site for her research and production laboratories. Here, Black women were taught in a diploma-granting program the application of the "Walker System" of hair care, and trained in marketing supplementary hair products and cosmetics manufactured in the Walker laboratories for which they received commissions.[46] Upon graduation these women were hired to work in their own shops that were a part of a chain of beauty parlors throughout the United States, the Caribbean, and South America.[47] Additionally by 1910, "the Walker company had employed some five thousand Black female agents around the world, and averaged revenues of about $1,000 a day, seven days a week."[48] Thus, Walker established new occupations beyond those of domestics and menial labor for Black women.

In 1917, after her attempt to purchase a home on Long Island, New York, was met with opposition from white residents, Walker had African American architect, Vertner W. Tandy design a $250,000 Georgian mansion that she had built at Irvington-on-the-Hudson. She reasoned that, "if moving into a white neighborhood would create a stir, she might as well choose the snootiest locality and make it a sensation."[49] This estate, specifically designed and built for the entertainment of African American artists and literati, housed $400,000 worth of international furnishings, and was dubbed Villa Lewaro by Enrico Caruso, the distinguished opera singer.[50] Walker "gave dinners, musicales, balls, and entertainments which at one time or another were attended by nearly every influential Negro in Black America."[51]

One of the first African American philanthropists, Walker during her lifetime contributed monies specifically to Black educational and other institutions of advancement that directly benefited women. Upon her death in 1919, Walker willed thousands of dollars to these institutions, as well as one hundred thousand to a West African girls school established by her; it was further mandated in her will that the Madame C. J. Walker Manufacturing Company always be managed by a woman.[52] The greater part of her wealth, Villa Lewaro, and Walker's Indiana Limestone adjoining brownstones in Harlem were left to her only daughter A'Leilia Walker Robinson, known by many as the "Mahogany Millionairess," who continued to provide a forum for artists and literati. The "Mahogany Millionairess" renovated the brownstones into a salon that she christened Dark Tower where she entertained an interracial group of such notables as, James Weldon Johnson, Zora Neale Hurston, Langston Hughes, Countee Cullen, Florence Mills, Charles Gilpin, Bruce Nugent, Aaron Douglas, Jean Toomer, Rudolph Fisher, Wallace Thurman and Carl Van Vechten up until 1930.[53]

Georgia Douglass Johnson (1877-1966) provided a forum in her Washington home for the literati, and made her own literary contributions to African American arts and letters, as did poet Anne Spencer who held a court of arts and letters at her home in Lynchburg, Virginia.[54] Zora Neale Hurston, anthropologist, novelist, folklorist and joint editor of *Fire!!* (1926), a radical cultural magazine for young

African American artists, worked for Fannie Hurst and was one of the beneficiaries of Nancy Cunard's Harlem Renaissance philanthropy. And Jessie Fauset, literary editor of *Crisis* (1919-1926), held dramatic contests to promote the development of African American drama and at the same time published her own literary works.[55] She simultaneously served first as literary editor, and later as managing editor of *Brownies' Book, A Monthly Magazine for the Children of the Sun* to "teach Universal Love and Brotherhood for all little folks--black and brown and yellow and white."[56] Incidentally, Fauset one of the first African American women to attend Cornell University (1901-1905), was a classical languages scholar and the first African American woman admitted to Phi Beta Kappa. These plaudits however, did not accord her insulation from discriminatory practices in mainstream American institutions, for like Coleman in Chicago, she too, "ran head-on into racism in the City of Brotherly Love, when she was refused a teaching position in the Philadelphia high schools" (1905).[57] Fauset went on to teach French and Latin in African American high schools in Baltimore and Washington, D. C. until she resigned to work for *Crisis* in 1919. Her education also included an M.A. from the University of Pennsylvania and study at the Sorbonne. Fauset attended the Second Pan-African Congress in Paris, at the same time Coleman attended, and wrote a two article account of this historical meeting for *The Crisis* in November and December, 1921.[58] As a novelist, and literary editor of *The Crisis*, Fauset's writing ventures encompassed fiction, non-fiction, and politics.

THE TRANSFORMATION OF AMERICAN ENTERTAINMENT

The focus on racial uplift differed between New York and Chicago. Whereas emphasis in New York was on the celebration of the Black Intelligentsia through the exhibition of their arts and letters, African American Chicagoans emphasized pragmatic economic self-sufficiency. Two of the largest African American communities in America at this time were located in Harlem, New York and on Chicago's Southside. These were the neighborhoods that the white elites frequented after dark, but more importantly they were the neighborhoods that Bessie Coleman frequented, occasionally with her friends Josephine Baker, Ethel Waters and Bill "Bojangles" Robinson.[59] The entertainment district of Southside Chicago is where she made contacts with people who were to be instrumental in her purchase of planes for barnstorming. It is also where the offices of Robert Abbott and Jessie Binga, her backers, were located. Even though the law of the land dictated that Blacks and whites should and could not interact (mix), the morally-minded, the socially-minded, the curious and adventuresome found ways to ignore these laws and in doing so established not only a new society of people, but new forms of entertainment that were to influence the cultural institutions of future generations. Coleman's entrance as an aviation entertainer was timely; audiences were enamored with African American Women performers and with suspenseful spectacle made possible by the augmentation of technology in theatre and film. She was an African American woman who chose to entertain in a mysterious technological machine--the airplane.

American mainstream entertainment was also undergoing a transformation in its efforts to embrace a transitional society of African American migrants, women, and non-English speaking immigrants now living side by side in the urban centers. During this search to accommodate and financially profit from the potentially vast audience, popular entertainment became a force with which to be reckoned. It was an entertainment borne out of the legitimate theatre, but yet not exactly embraced by that theatre. Robert C. Toll describes the national fervor for entertainment as an era when

> people clamored for professional entertainment. And they got it. Actors, actresses, musicians, singers, dancers, comedians, sharpshooters, chorus girls, acrobats, lion tamers, and many other types of barnstorming performers gave America the widest variety and greatest number of live shows ever seen in one country at one time.[60]

Melodrama became the theatrical genre that embraced each of these diverse forms of entertainment. Melodrama as practiced in the United States is a derivation of a combination of a form developed in France and Germany during the late Eighteenth century. In Germany the genre developed as a spoken passage accompanied by music, whereas in France the music was used to interpret the emotions of a silent character. As melodrama developed in this country, music was utilized behind the action to set the mood, interpret emotion and occasionally as incidental filler when combined with animal fare, acrobatics--people who flew through the air with the greatest of ease--and great escapes that caused the audience to hold its breath in suspense. The more suspenseful these programs became, the more suspense the audiences demanded.

Since the earliest theatrical productions, American theatre practitioners had been in search of a quintessentially American drama. They wanted a drama that reflected thematic and structural concerns native to the American experience. While this type of theatre might indeed reflect the influence of European precursors, it was to be both distinguishable from and aesthetically equal in merit to its source. Thespian, Edwin Forrest, construed the injunction for theatre native to the American soil literally, by mandating Native American subjects. He offered a $500 prize "for writers to submit tragedies in five acts in which the hero or principal character 'shall be an aboriginal of this country.'"[61] The competition was also a fundamental effort in moving American artists and society away from their Eurocentric perspective of what constituted art. Until then, American theatre had relied on adaptations of European scripts. Forrest's search generated playscripts such as *Metamora,* a "romantic melodrama, with all of the violence, the action, the love, and the sentiment that melodrama of this time required."[62]

The early melodramatic stage produced a variety of dramas for a diverse audience. All kinds of performances were housed under one roof, so that audiences in the 1830s might see drama, circus, opera, and dance on the same bill. It remains manifestly clear, however, that American drama gained its popularity neither from European adaptations, nor from lyric poetry, but from the inclusion of indigenous American characters into a sensational melodramatic format. Theatre evolved from the legitimate stage into circuses, tent shows, vaudeville, and variety in an effort to provide entertainment for the new generation of non-English speaking immigrants. As the technological age produced automobiles, trains, and airplanes, they too were included in melodramatic scripts to enhance suspense and excitement; all were to develop in importance during the early twenties.

By mid-nineteenth century, melodrama embraced urban ethnic characters to become a genre that still remains the most popular theatre genre in American entertainment, perhaps with the exception of musicals.[63] For example, during the period in question as the urban centers expanded, melodramas began to include African American, Irish, and Jewish characters. As early as 1859 Dion Boucicault (1822-1890), produced a melodrama *The Octoroon* (1859), on the American stage, that features the unrequited love of a white man for an African American woman, and singularly presents an African American, an Indian, and Yankee replete with dialects.

Also during the mid-nineteenth century, however, American entertainment evolved along lines distinctly race-conscious. Racial and ethnic caricatures were used for levity; and not only of African Americans, but of Irish, German, Jewish, and others--in fact whichever underclass, *à-la-mode*, was in too politically weak a position to protest. Thomas "Daddy" Rice (1808-1860), Phineas Taylor Barnum (1810-1891), George L. Aiken (?-1876), and Tony Pastor (1837-1908), all had their fingers on the entertainment pulse of America's new masses when they established their respective forms of entertainment. All were grounded in popular entertainment and all utilized the image of African Americans even when the actual person was excluded.

Thomas "Daddy" Rice created a completely new genre in American entertainment when he first jumped "Jim Crow" (the title later applied to segregation laws) on a New York stage in black-face, buffooning African Americans in 1832.[64] "Jim Crowism" became a sensational act to be repeated time and time again, with thunderous applause from a segregated society. And little did America know that the Black man's deformity would shape the disfigurement of the Nation for so long a time.[65] From this single event an entire genre was developed and endured into the early twentieth century under the guise of minstrelsy; eventually it took its place in film.

Phineas Taylor Barnum established the circus as an American institution (1835), with the exhibition of Joice Heath, supposedly a 161-year-old African American former slave woman touted by Barnum to be George Washington's nurse. Harriet Beecher Stowe wrote the controversial literary work *Uncle Tom's Cabin* (1852), as a serious, if sentimental anti-slavery novel. Although Stowe opposed its adaptation for the stage, George L. Aiken wrote the melodrama *Uncle Tom's Cabin* (1852, three-act; 1853, six-act), based on her novel.[66] It became ensconced for more than half a century on the American stage as the most popular melodrama ever written, where it was continually revised for performance in almost every *genre* implemented and ultimately was sapped of its anti-slavery message. This melodrama was so popular by 1899 that it permeated American entertainment nationwide with five hundred stock companies designated as "Tom Shows;" and was also performed throughout Europe.[67] Even P.T. Barnum produced a prototype devoid of any political sentiments, but loaded with melodramatic devices. He publicized it as a show that made no effort to "foolishly and unjustly elevate the negro [sic] above the white man in intellect or morals," but rather presented "a true picture of negro life in the South."[68] According to David Grimsted, Barnum's version was Aikens' most formidable competitor.

Tony Pastor, formerly of Barnum's circus, established the vaudeville stage in 1881 in an effort to provide clean, healthy entertainment for the entire family. All of these events resulted in a synthesized transformation of American society in general.

Vaudeville grew out of the need to entertain the masses. Pastor continued the American tradition of eclectic entertainment by presenting several genres borne of the theatre on one stage in a single evening. In addition to a forum that included "all of the artistic resources of every branch of the theatre--grand opera, the drama, pantomime, choreography, concert, symphony, farce, and all of the kindred fields of stage entertainment", Pastor featured several ethnic and racial type actors and characters, reflective of his patrons who attended the Palace theatre for entertainment.[69] This fact doubtless enhanced the popularity of vaudeville. Popular entertainment can verifiably trace its lineage from a melding of legitimate theatre and innovative novelties. As Garff B. Wilson has concluded:

> The circus borrowed blackface entertainment from minstrelsy, horseback performances from the equestrian drama, and variety acts from vaudeville. Minstrelsy borrowed its "olio" from vaudeville. Burlesque patterned its show after minstrelsy and introduced song and dance numbers from vaudeville. Vaudeville adopted blackface numbers from minstrelsy, leg shows from burlesque, and acrobatics and animal acts from the circus. In fact, all the types of popular theatre are basically a series of specialities strung together in a characteristic way. Each emphasizes a slightly different specialty, but each aims to satisfy the tastes of a polyglot audience by providing novel and varied entertainment which is easily understood.[70]

Musical entertainment was one avenue by which African Americans could and did successfully thresh out a livelihood. Although they became visible on the professional minstrel stage during the latter part of the 1860s, by 1890 some African Americans had begun to wrest their theatrical destiny from minstrelsy on the musical stage with the ushering in of *The Creole Show*.[71] This production was a departure from "all-masculine blackface minstrels," in that it featured women on stage and was the first production to demonstrate that an all Black production could attract an audience. Several musical shows gradually deviating from the minstrel subject and structure were to follow; among them *Oriental America*, the first all-Black company to appear on Broadway, the first to include operatic selections among its musical numbers and to feature in its cast trained musicians such as Rosamond Johnson.[72] During the great migration, of which Coleman took part, when African Americans found themselves unemployed in the North, many utilized their entertainment skills developed during their days of enslavement by raising their voices in song, tapping their feet in a rhythmic beat, and clowning their way onto the minstrel, vaudeville, and legitimate stages to stardom after emancipation. Daphne Duval Harrison writes of this period that,

> the demand for entertainment in the hammocks of the country mill towns and the avenues of southern and northern cities

came from a black population that was on the move
geographically and economically at the turn of the century.[73]

Music and theatre became an integral part of this entertainment that
was rapidly changing to encompass a society constantly in transition
from the late nineteenth and into the twentieth century. Black music
continued to evolve from plantation music--spirituals and work songs
into urban music--blues into jazz. As it found a home in theatre, it
became a merging force that integrated Blacks and whites, women and
men, upper and lower classes.

Individual African American women had received international
recognition on the recital stage at least eleven years before the
endorsement of the Emancipation Proclamation, and almost forty years
before the advent of *The Creole Show*. Among these women were
Elizabeth Taylor Greenfield (1824-1876), a soprano dubbed the Black
Swan, who presented a command performance to Queen Victoria at
Buckingham Palace in 1853; Sisseretta Jones (1869-1933), billed as
Black Patti had performed for many years receiving rave critical reviews
from the national press by the time she was invited by President
Harrison to sing at the White House in 1892.[74] It was also through
music and theatre that African American culture found its way into
white society.

Ernest Hogan, songwriter and veteran of the minstrel stage,
introduced the "Cakewalk" to Caucasians in a production entitled
Clorindy: The Origin of the Cakewalk (1898). Will Marion Cook
(1869-1944) created the story, and Paul Laurence Dunbar, whose works
were inspirational to Coleman, provided the libretto and lyrics for this
production that featured handsome couples comprised of Black women
in attractive gowns and Black men minus blackfaced makeup executing
this dance that was to become popular in white society.[75] The
Charleston an African American dance surpassed the Cakewalk in
popularity by becoming the signature dance of the 1920s. Again, it was
introduced to those outside of the African American community from
the legitimate stage when it was performed in the musical *Runnin'*
Wild (1923).[76] (Even the Lindy Hop, in celebration of Charles
Augustus Lindbergh's Transatlantic flight (1926-27), although not
introduced on stage, was generated in the Black community).[77] If
Lindbergh knew of Coleman, which was most probable, his racist
attitudes regarding African Americans and aviation obviated his public
recognition of her activities. "Almost every major jazz orchestra of the
1920s played for theater shows whenever they were not touring the
dance halls;" and several dancers from various Black musical
productions were hired to give private lessons to individual white
people, as well as to entire chorus lines during this period.[78] Theatre
then, functioning as conveyor of Black culture to white America, also

dissolved the barriers of segregation in some institutions. As Black entertainers became more in demand, it was necessary for them to have organized scheduling for impending engagements.

The T.O.B.A. established around 1907, who handled Coleman's air show engagements for a short time, was the largest booking company for African American performers on the Black vaudeville circuit. While the acronym formally stood for Theatre Owners Booking Association, it was informally designated by the performers "tough on Black actors" because of the grueling, unrealistic bookings scheduled predominately in the segregated South where they could not eat in restaurants, stay in hotels or even use the restrooms. They had to perform in one town, and frequently, immediately after a performance, drive all night in order to arrive at the next engagement. The theatres on this circuit featuring Black vaudeville entertainment comprised of "comedy, circus acts, dramatic scenes, and pure vaudeville hokum as well as singing and dancing" were located in large Southern and Midwestern cities that included,

Jacksonville, Florida, to Little Rock, Arkansas, from Kansas City, Missouri, to Bessemer, Alabama, and while there was no official T.O.B.A. theater in New York, black artists performed at the Seventh Avenue Lafayette Theatre and at the Alhambra.[79]

Significantly, this circuit was the training ground for the African American women who were transmitting the Blues to mainstream America via "race recordings" during the early 1920s. Mamie Smith (no relation to Bessie) recorded the first blues for Okey in November, 1920; "it sold seventy-five thousands copies in a month."[80] Ma Rainey (1886-1939) "Mother of the Blues" toured with her Rabbit Foot Minstrels, carnivals, tent shows and circuses where Bessie Smith "Empress of the Blues" and Rainey's protégée met her and began her own career as a youngster in show business. Likewise Josephine Baker "the toast of Paris," began her career as Bessie Smith's protégée on the same circuit; all were to eventually perform on the legitimate stage.[81] Alberta Hunter and earlier Bessie Coleman were also booked with T.O.B.A. Hunter's performances as a vocalist, of course, fall squarely within accepted definitions of entertainment. Coleman's bookings, however, demonstrate to what extent she too was regarded by her contemporaries as an entertainer: she booked lecture tours through T.O.B.A., especially at movie theatres which were featuring screenings of newsreel footage of her stuntflying.

Entertainers on this circuit were paid poorly if they were paid at all, they played one-night stands in rural and urban districts, with second-

class transportation in over-crowded trains, were accommodated in cheap
hotels, frequently worked without costumes and sets, and relied on
unknown resident theatre bands for music.[82] Sometimes headliners
faired better, but this was the standard treatment for most.

The road company of the musical production *Shuffle Along* had
endured all of these inequities and more by the time the curtain went up
in the 63rd Street Theatre May 23, 1921. Florenz Ziegfeld and George
White among others hired African American dancers from the chorus
line of *Shuffle Along* to teach white women jazz steps. Eubie Blake,
Noble Sissle and occasionally their orchestra were frequently hired after
the show to entertain wealthy white people for their private parties at
home.[83] *Shuffle Along,* then, reflected in both its various parts and its
composite structure the social and cultural transitions of American
musical theatre and of the African American from southern and rural to
northern and urban. It integrated elements of the European Operetta
popularly employed in American musical theatre with those of African
American blues, and jazz, in a plot that represented rural and urban
characters breaking into dance on stage. Robert Kimball and William
Bolcom philosophically observed that although *Shuffle Along* was
comprised of a series of parts that appeared to be unrelated, "...the unity
is something like the unity in plurality of America itself--held together
by its very disparateness and many-faceted character, in a way that any
hierarchical order would violate."[84] African American music played a
vital role in the integration of races, sexes and classes; it was the music
primarily of the speakeasies, cabarets, and the stage. African American
artists and entertainers were also responsible for amicable relationships
among the races in France, so that by the time Bessie Coleman traveled
to France she was treated congenially.

AFRICAN AMERICANS AND THE
FRENCH CONNECTION

While American entertainment had acquired its long sought
distinctive cast, it still admitted some European influence, particularly
via France. The "French connection" to American arts and letters had
been established since the late eighteenth century when American
dramatist William Dunlap (1766-1839) father of American drama,
adapted Guilbert de Pixérécort's French melodramas to the American
stage.[85] The initiation of French exposure to the talent of African
Americans however, probably began around the mid-Nineteenth century
with sculptor, Eugene Warbourg (c. 1825-67) who traveled to Europe in
1852. He produced several episodes of *Uncle Tom's Cabin* in a series of
bas-reliefs under commission from the Duchess of Sutherland; and
represented the State of Louisiana at the Paris Exposition in 1867.[86]

Robert S. Duncanson (1817-1872) a landscape artist, toured the French art salons during 1853 under sponsorship from the Anti-Slavery League and also illustrated *Uncle Tom and Little Eva* (1853), commissioned by James Francis Conover editor of the Detroit *Tribune*.[87] Edmonia Lewis (1845-1890) the first Black American woman sculptor succeeded these two artists with her expatriation to Rome in 1865. Lewis sculpted in marble adopting the Neoclassical style prevalent during this period and received international acclaim by becoming one of the highest paid sculptors in the world for her renditions of "John Brown," "Abraham Lincoln" (1867), and "Forever Free" (1867) in celebration of the Thirteenth Amendment, among many other works.[88] Henry Ossawa Tanner (1859-1937) a painter, arrived in Paris in 1891, and actually established residence in that city until his death. He received honorable mention from the Paris Salon in 1896, a Gold Medal in 1897, and was eventually elected to the French National Academy.[89] The excellence of these artists undoubtedly made it possible for other African American artists searching for artistic freedom, to later be accepted in the Paris salons.

Subsequently, African American presence during World War I made an indelible mark on French society through music. James Reese Europe (1881-1919), a lieutenant in the United States Army during World War I, was a renowned conductor, who traveled throughout France and Europe during a tour of duty with his 369th regiment band introducing African American music. This regiment played for French and American troops behind the front lines, in hospitals, camps, and for civilians as well.[90] According to Eubie Blake he was laying the ground work in pursuit of his dream "to restore the Negro to the American stage" when he was murdered.[91] Eubie Blake further praises James Reese Europe as a person who was indispensable to African American musicians because

...he did as much for them as Martin Luther King did for the rest of the Negro people. He set up a way to get them jobs-- the Clef Club--and he made them get paid more. He tried to get as much for them as whites, and sometimes he could and sometimes he couldn't. And all the rich white people loved him. He used to get *all* the jobs for those millionaire parties, and of course we went along.[92]

Al Rose, Blake's biographer, characterized the pre-World War I era as

a time in American social history when, with competition glorified in every area of human activity, the compulsion

glorified among the very rich to outdo one another in lavish
and extravagant social functions reached a peak. Vernon and
Irene Castle danced their way to immortality as they taught the
world Jim Europe's Castle Walk and the variety of ballroom
steps his music accompanied. It was inevitable that his young
buddies Sissle and Blake should become well-known society
entertainers along the Eastern seaboard. They played for
Goulds, Dodges, Schwabs, Wanamakers--anybody who was
anybody in the *haut monde*.[93]

Noble Sissle, of *Shuffle Along* fame, was Europe's assistant and one of
the musicians. Thus by the time Robert Abbott encouraged Coleman to
travel to France to learn to fly, he was quite confident that she would be
accepted.

MELODRAMA, TECHNOLOGY, BARNSTORMING AND FILM

Throughout this discussion one element that certainly belongs to
the legitimate stage continues to appear as the foundation of American
entertainment forms since its infancy. That element is melodrama. As
stated earlier, melodrama introduced patriotic, ethnic and racial characters
to the legitimate stage; it provided a structure of good versus evil with
which the masses could identify, urban versus rural, aristocracy versus
proletarian; and all of this reflected the concerns of a society in
transition. Bessie Coleman conformed to this ambiance; with roots in
Southern rural United States, performing in the urban North, and in
taking advantage of a fairly new and suspicious machine--the airplane--
adapting it to her performance.

By the time World War I produced a surplus of airplanes, the
fascination with airplanes combined with entertainment forged a new
form--barnstorming. By the early 1920s barnstorming, initially in
reference to itinerant actors, had become primarily synonymous with
unemployed former World War I fighter pilots who flew surplus army
aircraft to entertain the public. Barnstorming transcended the boundaries
of the legitimate stage into the vast expanse of an infinite horizon. It
was precisely this type of melodramatic spectacle wedded with
technology that contributed to the decline in popularity of the
legitimate stage, as cinema began to flourish.

As the nation was transformed from an agrarian to an industrial
society and from rural to urban, melodrama also incorporated the
technology that had become an integral part of this society. The

entertainment world merged with the technological world with the adoption of a variety of complicated stage machinery.

> As the taste for sensational novelties grew, productions became increasingly elaborate and expensive. Metropolitan stages became more complicated with bridges, traps, elevators, moving platforms, and all kinds of paraphernalia for producing fires, floods, explosions, and all manner of astounding displays. The two-dimensional scenery was replaced by built-up solid pieces making the sets substantial and difficult to move.[94]

Gas lighting, instead of candles and oil lamps, employed in *Mazepa,* an equestrian melodrama in 1832, maximized spectacle through three dimensional detail; the elevator stage was inaugurated by Steele McKaye in 1880 shortly after the invention of the elevator; the telegraph was utilized to tap out an S. O. S. in *Across the Continent* or *Scenes from New York* during the 1860s; the electric light, developed by Thomas Edison in 1879 was first employed in a production of Gilbert and Sullivan's *Patience* in 1881; an oncoming train was employed for suspense in Daly's *Under the Gaslight* (1867) as the audience sat spellbound waiting to see if the hero tied to the railroad tracks would be rescued before a train sent him into oblivion. Even P. T. Barnum exploited the public's fermenting curiosity with flight when on July 26, 1874 he featured the airship "Barnum," a hot air balloon, ascending from his theatre now known as Madison Square Garden.[95]

Motion pictures rivaled the legitimate stage on several levels. First, the nickel admission was twenty cents less than a ticket to the theatre. Secondly, the 1890 audiences who had begun to demand more spectacle were comprised of immigrants. A picture in the movies was "worth more than a thousand words" for immigrants who did not speak English.[96] The films provided spectacle filled with suspense much cheaper, and in larger than life images that were more believable than could be sketched by the live actors on a stage distanced from the audience by an orchestra pit and surrounded by a proscenium arch. Movie moguls pandered to this audience and films became more and more sensational. The increasing reliance on technology, in fact, spawned the growth of the film industry.

It is no coincidence that the *Perils of Pauline* serials were an early sensation in film, and that Mary Pickford made the transition from the stage into films to become "America's Sweetheart" as the highest paid actress in the world during the early twenties. The sharp contrast between her passive, angelic purity, on the one hand, and the base depravity of the villain menacing her, on the other hand, was easily understood and relished by an uneducated audience. Moreover, that extreme contrast lent itself especially well to cinematic treatment, heightening the intensity of suspense through closeup shots of characters in fear and terror, camera angles emphasizing impending doom and disaster, and realistic special effects.

Until the 1920s, a dominant elite group had controlled the offerings of both highbrow and popular entertainment. While popular entertainment admittedly and unabashedly appealed to the masses, it was nevertheless produced by the elite group with the money to bankroll spectacular performances. When film became popular, according to Geoffrey Perrett, "Hollywood had created a new elite, a democratic aristocracy" ... that "displaced the older elite that had dominated the popular imagination through its wealth and arrogance--Rockefeller, Vanderbilt, Gould, Morgan, and the like."[97]

The entrance of cinema as a serious contender for the populist dollar changed that relationship, by distracting its controllers' interests. That is, the controlling group did not discard its investments in the live popular stage. Nevertheless, it seemed less concerned about what subjects or themes were presented on stage than were presented in the newly-emergent cinema. The movie theatre, both as a novelty and in its capacity to represent images in a larger-than-life format, seemed to have a greater capacity to shape more people's perceptions of themselves through catharsis and resolution than did live theatre. In other words, it provided a new and completely open field through which women, immigrants and African Americans could be instructed about ways in which they should perceive their own natures, powers, rights, and avenues of expression.

Bessie Coleman recognized the importance of establishing an image of herself, as an African American woman, in any media available during her era. By the end of her life, she was aggressively and adamantly seeking a producer to immortalize her life and achievements on film. Even before she put her thoughts about film into writing, she could and did selectively utilize the contrasts and sensationalism which audiences found so appealing in cinematic melodrama. She was petite and attractive, and had her costumes tailored to cast her as a heroic figure through their quasi-military trappings, but at the same time fashionably cut to emphasize her feminine figure.[98] Thus when she stood next to her aircraft at the beginning of a performance, she seemed both exceedingly small and exceedingly brave. When she soared into the air, and flew awe-inspiring maneuvers, she asserted her control and mastery over the machine, which seemed impossibly large, complex and sophisticated to her audiences. She appeared to exercise command over the natural elements themselves, floating and spiralling and pulling out of a dive at the absolute last moment before a crash. Onlookers who had been disarmed by her graceful femininity, and who had equated that grace with the helplessness of melodrama heroines like Mary Pickford, were forced to acknowledge that the death-defying pilot swooping and spiraling in the heavens was, indeed, a woman. Thus Coleman subverted the image of woman as fragile and passive. Further, she proved her point in person, by flying live performances, leaving no doubt about how much of her personal risk was real, and how much the creation of special effects. She saw film as an adjunct media for preserving her exploits, rather than as a primary vehicle.

As discussed in Chapter IV, Coleman's performances embodied the heroic; they were both urban, and rural; and they were fashionable and simple. Coleman adopted a fairy tale quality by aligning herself with Joan of Arc, and had costumes made to reflect this. In fact all of her costumes were "patriotic" and designed especially for each performance. And like Joan of Arc she had a purpose--hers was not for self-aggrandizement, but to establish an aviation school for African Americans.

For a culture already primed for spectacle that began on the legitimate stage, it is no surprise that barnstorming became extraordinarily popular. Here, the audience could actually speak with the performers before they went up in the plane. The more adventuresome could for $1 to $5 take a ride in the barnstormers' airplane. The audience witnessed death-defying acts that were not staged--there were no trap-doors to ensure a safe escape. Performers could, and sometimes did, crash to their deaths.

Coleman embraced an entire spectrum of white women, non-English speaking immigrants, and of course racially proud African Americans, both as members of her audience, and as newspaper readers who found her exploits thrilling and inspiring. Women were clamoring for the vote which they gained in 1921. This achievement brought women into the public realm that had formerly belonged to men. Coleman was also devoted to undermining the legend of *Uncle Tom* which is evidenced in her statements as a young girl (Chapter III) and in the actual christening of her hangar Uncle Tom (Chapter IV). Audiences did not have to speak English to understand her performances; some women were delighted to see another woman engaged in challenging endeavors; and melodrama--along with an optimistic national spirit in the Roaring Twenties--had already stimulated the public appetite for adventure.

Bessie Coleman embodied the best qualities of the Black Nationalists and the club women. Coleman was a member of this race-conscience African American educated elite. Although she did not complete college, she was educated up through her freshman year at the Colored Agricultural and Normal University in Langston, Oklahoma.[99] It is evidenced by many of her decisions regarding her career in aviation that she was not illiterate, nor did she cease to learn because of financial hardship, but continued to educate herself throughout her life by reading and keeping up with current events.[100] Coleman was an entrepreneur; she had documentaries made of her exploits when film became popular, and was making arrangements to have movies made for entertainment of her barnstorming exploits during the year she died.[101] She, like Barnum and Pastor, exploited the times and gave the audience what they wanted. Even though "Negrotarian" philanthropy became a popular institution, Coleman farsightedly insisted upon tapping into the resources of the African American community by seeking financial assistance from Robert Abbott and Jesse Binga, the two African American philanthropists located in Chicago who financially backed Coleman's trip to France.

Although Bessie Coleman did not hold the formal credentials that would have entitled her to *de facto* membership in Du Bois's "Talented Tenth," she attended in 1921 the Second Pan African Congress, a meeting of the elite of African descent. While there is no evidence that she was a "Club Woman," she was eulogized by Ida B. Wells-Barnett, one of the most preeminent club women of her day. Bessie Coleman was clearly one in spirit with these women. Although documentation of her interactions with African American women in Chicago and New York is scant, Wells-Barnett's eulogy suggests that Coleman had cultivated and maintained a sisterly support network. Coleman's attitude and actions manifested the race-consciousness of her pursuit to build an aviation school for the education of African Americans. At the same time that Bessie Coleman was politically engaged in race uplift, she never lost the elemental exuberance and sheer joy of being alive that characterized all her undertakings. Finding in the rapidly changing field of popular entertainment of the 1920s a vitality similar to her own, she flew down that runway of entertainment in an airplane, in an attempt to enter mainstream America and to bring other African Americans in with her.

This then, was the scenario of the United States between 1896, the year Bessie Coleman was born, and 1926 the year of her fatal crash. Politically, World War I transformed American societal attitudes and behavior. Racial consciousness was at a peak in the African American communities. White people's peculiar interest in everything black provided the necessary stage for Coleman's performances. Indeed, this rapidly changing society forced people to review and reassess their existence. This was a period of disillusionment in the human condition, but at the same time that disillusionment engendered an intensity to celebrate the human condition. Youth were imbued with an attitude of living for the moment; including a drive for different outlets of entertainment. Segregation laws in many cases forced African Americans to search for alternative avenues into the American mainstream; entertainment was one of these avenues. New genres of authentic American entertainment were developing. Minstrels, circuses, vaudeville, film, and barnstorming became the popular entertainment for the masses.

Bessie Coleman was popular as an aviatrix because, rather than be defeated by restrictions of American society, she adapted her skills to give the general public what they wanted. Furthermore, Coleman provided a tenacious role model of courage and daring that African Americans were proud to follow during a decade in American history when laws and practices were designed to defeat their progress.

Notes

1. "Texas Negro Girl Becomes Able Aviatrix," *Houston Post Dispatch,* 7 May 1925: 4.

2. Florette Henri, *Black Migration: Movement North 1900-1920* (New York: Anchor Books, 1976) 12.

3. See Ida B. Wells, *A Red Record: Tabulated Statistics and Alleged Causes of Lynchings in the United States, 1892-1893-1894* (1894, Chicago; New York: Arno Press, 1971).

4. Henri 145.

5. Henri 150-152.

6. For Example, *Fire in the Flint* (1924) by Walter White, is a novel about an African American who believes he can ignore the race problem in Georgia because he is a successful M.D., until the rape of his sister and the lynching of his brother forces him to realize that all Blacks must confront the problem. Other works of the period with similar themes include plays Rachel (1916), *A Sunday Morning in the South* (1925), and novels *There is Confusion* (1924), *The Walls of Jericho* (1928), *The Blacker the Berry* (1929), and *Not Without Laughter* (1930).

7. E. David Cronon, *Black Moses: The Story of Marcus Garvey and the Universal Improvement Association* (1955; Madison: The University of Wisconsin Press, 1969) 70, 69; Emmett J. Scott served as Special Assistant to the Secretary of War during WW I, and documented the discrimination and prejudice endured by Blacks serving overseas at the hands of white American soldiers in his book entitled, *The American Negro in the World War* (Washington, D.C., 1919; Erroll Hill provides the most comprehensive documentation on the life of Henrietta Vinton Davis in, "From Artist to Activist," *Shakespeare in Sable: A History of Black Shakespearean Actors* (Amherst: The University of Massachusetts Press, 1984) 64-79. For a more complete listing of distinguished U.N.I.A. membership see Theodore G. Vincent, "Appendix 2, Prominent Garveyites," *Black Power and the Garvey Movement* (San Francisco: Ramparts Press, 1976) 267-270.

8. Black is here employed in reference to all international descendants of Africans, including for example West Indians, Hispanics and indigenous Africans as well as African Americans. African Americans on the other hand, refers exclusively to those of African descent who are United States citizens and may be interchangeable with Negro, Black, Aframerican and Afro-American dependant on the dictates of historical reference.

9. John Hope Franklin, *From Slavery to Freedom: A History of Negro Americans* (New York: Alfred A. Knopf, 1968) 490.

10. Geoffrey Perrett, America in the Twenties: A History (New York: Simon & Schuster, Inc., 1982) 239.

11. *Crisis*, XIX (1919-20) 241. Elliot Rudwick. *W. E. B. DuBois: Voice of the Black Protest Movement* (Chicago: University of Illinois Press, 1960) 237.

12. David Levering-Lewis, *When Harlem Was In Vogue* (New York: Alfred A. Knopf, 1981) 98.

13. The extent to which African Americans themselves succumbed to this buyer's market can be seen both in Wallace Thurman's satirical novel, *Infants of the Spring* (1932) and Langston Hughes' autobiography *The Big Sea* (1940).

14. Alain Locke, ed., foreword, *The New Negro* (1925; New York: Atheneum, 1980) xvi.

15. Francis Scott Fitzgerald, quoted in *The Readers's Encyclopedia*, (1948; New York: Thomas Y. Crowell Company, 1965) 352.

16. Langston Hughes, "The Negro Artist and the Racial Mountain," *The Nation* 23 June 1926: 694.

17. Darwin Turner, *Black Drama In America: An Anthology* (Connecticut: Fawcett Publications, Inc., 1971) 3.

18. Langston Hughes, *The Big Sea: An Autobiography* (1940; New York: Hill and Wang, 12th printing, 1981) 224.

19. Langston Hughes and Milton Meltzer, *Black Magic: A Pictorial History of Black Entertainers in America* (New York: Bonanza Books, 1967) 97-105; Henry T. Sampson, *Blacks in Blackface: A Source Book on early Black Musical Shows* (New Jersey: The Scarecrow Press, Inc., 1980) 23.

20. Fannie Barrier Williams, "The Club Movement Among Colored Women of America," *A New Negro for a New Century: An Accurate and Up-To-Date Record of the Upward Struggles of the Negro Race*, eds. Booker T. Washington, N. B. Wood, and Fannie Barrier Williams (1900, Chicago; New York: Arno Press and The New York Times, 1969) 393.

21. Flexner 191-196; Williams 397; For more comprehensive discussions on the adversarial relationships between African American and white women see Rosalyn Terborg-Penn, "Discrimination Against Afro-American Women in the Women's Movement, 1830-1920," *The Afro-American Woman: Struggles and Images*, eds. Sharon Harley and Rosalyn Terborg-Penn (New York: Kennikat Press, 1978) 17-27; Paula Giddings, "To Choose Again Freely," Chapter III; and "The Quest for Woman Suffrage (Before World War I)," Chapter VII, *When and Where I Enter: The Impact of Black Women on Race and Sex in America* (New York: William Morrow and Company, Inc., 1984); and Aileen Kraditor, *The Ideas of the Women Suffrage Movement, 1899-1929* (New York: Anchor Books/Doubleday, 1971).

22. Williams 382-383.

23. Williams 421-424.

24. Langston Hughes, *Fight for Freedom: The Story of the NAACP* (New York: W. W. Norton & Company, Inc., 1962) 22.

25. Dorothy Sterling, "Ida B. Wells: Voice of a People," *Black Foremothers: Three Lives* (New York: The Feminist Press, 1979) 78-80.

26. Edgar A. Toppin, *A Biographical History of Blacks in America Since 1528* (1969; New York: David McKay Company, Inc., The Christian Science Publishing Society, 1971) 447; Rebecca Stiles Taylor, "A Review of the Lives of Three Magnificent Women [Ethel Wilson Ransom, Ida B. Wells-Barnett, and Elizabeth Lindsey Davis]," *The Chicago Defender* 15 January 1938: 17; Flexner 192-193.

27. Ida B. Wells, *A Red Record: Tabulated Statistics and Alleged Causes of Lynchings in the United States, 1892-1893-1894* (1894, Chicago; New York: Arno Press, 1971).

28. Ida B. Wells-Barnett, *Crusade for Justice: The Autobiography of Ida B. Wells-Barnett*, ed. Alfreda Duster (Chicago: University of Chicago Press, 1970) 345-347; Paula Giddings, *When and Where I Enter: The Impact of Black Women on Race and Sex in America* (New York: William Morrow and Company, Inc., 1984) 126-128.

29. Mrs. E. C. Hobson and Mrs. C. E. Hopkins, "Report Concerning the Colored Women of the South", quoted in Eleanor Flexnor, *Century of Struggle: The Woman's Rights Movement in the United States* (1959; Massachusetts: The Belknap Press of Harvard University Press, 1982) 191; Williams 396-397.

30. Giddings 127; Kraditor, *Ideas of Woman Suffrage*, 167-168; Flexnor, 317-318.

31. Giddings 22-23.

32. Sterling, 71.

33. Sterling, 68.

34. Wells-Barnett, 289-295. For a comprehensive account of the Pekin Theatre see Henry T. Sampson, "Famous Black Theatres," *Blacks in Blackface: A Source Book on Early Black Musical Shows* (New Jersey: The Scarecrow Press, Inc., 1980) 115-119.

35. Flexner 195.

36. Sterling, "Mary Church Terrell," *Black Foremothers*, 132-133.

37. Sterling, 146-147, 153.

38. Mary Church Terrell, *A Colored Woman in a White World* (Washington, D.C.: Ransdell Inc. Publishers, 1940) 205; Flexner 195.

39. Sterling 131.

40. Bettye Collier-Thomas, *Black Women In America: Contributors to Our Heritage* (Washington, D. C.: The Bethune Museum-Archives, Inc., institutions of the National Council of Negro

Women, 1983) N. pag. For further comments regarding this proposed monument see W.E.B. DuBois, "The Black Mother (1912)," *The W. E. B. Du Bois Reader,* ed. Meyer Weinberg (New York: Harper & Row, Publishers, 1970) 101.

41.Wilhelmena S. Robinson, *International Library of Negro Life and History: Historical Negro Biographies* (New York: Publishers Company, Inc., under the auspices of The Association for the Study of Negro Life and History, 1967) 128.

42. "Mrs. Mary Talbert is Dead," *The Chicago Defender* 20 October, 1923: 1; James Weldon Johnson, *Black Manhattan* (1930, Knopf; New York: Arno Press and The New York Times, 1968) 56.

43. Edgar A. Toppin, *A Biographical History of Blacks in America Since 1528* (New York: David McKay Company, Inc., 1971) 435.

44. Ottley 172; Toppin 435-36.

45. Ottley, 172.

46. Toppin, 436; Giddings, 188.

47. Giddings 187-188.

48. Giddings, 188.

49. Ottley, 172.

50. Ottley, 172.

51. Ottley, 172.

52. Giddngs 188; Ottley 173.

53. Ottley, 174. These brownstones later housed the Schomberg Collection of Negro Literature and History, purchased by the Carnegie Corporation of New York in 1926, and eventually became a permanent branch of the New York Public Library.

54. Winona L. Fletcher, "Georgia Douglas Johnson (1886-1966)," *Dictionary of Literary Biography 51: Afro-American Writers from the Harlem Renaissance to 1940* (Detroit: Gale Research, 1987) 153-163; Gloria T. Hull, *Color, Sex and Poetry: Three Women Writers of the Harlem Renaissance* (Bloomington: Indiana University Press, 1987) 6, 165-166; Chauncey E. Spencer, *Who Is Chauncey Spencer?* Detroit: Broadside Press, 1975; Enoch P. Waters, "Little Air Show Becomes A National Crusade," *American Diary: A Personal History of the Black Press* (Chicago: Path Press, Inc., 1987) 200; Ann Allen Shockley, *Afro-American Women Writers 1746-1933* (New York: New American Library, 1988) 411.

55. Fauset wrote four novels between 1924 and 1933: *There is Confusion* (1924); *Plum Bum* (1929); *The Chinaberry Tree* (1931); and *Comedy, American Style* (1933). Her literary works portray the lives of upper and middle class African Americans; demonstrating that their aspirations, cultural and social activities are not that different from their white American counterparts.

56. Ann Allen Shockley, "The New Negro Movement 1924-1933," *Afro-American Women Writers 1746-1933 An Anthology and Critical Guide* (New York: New American Library, 1989) 417.

57. Shockley 416.

58.Arthur P. Davis, *From the Dark Tower: Afro-American Writers 1900-1960* (1974; Washington, D.C.: Howard University Press, 1982) 91.

59. Marion Coleman, personal interview with Elizabeth Hadley Freydberg and Kathleen Collins, 12 January 1985.

60. Robert C. Toll, *The Entertainment Machine: American Show Business in the Twentieth Century* (New York: Oxford University Press, 1982) 6.

61.Dale Shaw, *Titans of the American Stage: Edwin Forrest, the Booths, the O'Neills* (Philadelphia: The Westminster Press, MCMLXXI) 31 .

62. Walter J. Meserve, *An Outline History of American Drama* (New Jersey: Littlefield, Adams & Co., 1965) 78.

63. Oscar Brockett, *The Theatre: An Introduction, Historical Edition* (1964; Holt, Rinehart, and Winston, Inc., 1979) 329.

64. C. Vann Woodward, *The Strange Career of Jim Crow* (1955; New York, 1974) establishes this as the date of origin for Thomas D. Rice's song and dance, "Jim Crow." He further indicates that although this term became an adjective by 1838, the origin of its reference to African Americans is "lost in obscurity." 7n. Also see Robert C. Toll, *Blacking Up: The Minstrel Show in Nineteenth-Century America* (New York: Oxford University Press, 1974) 28, indicates this as the date that Rice first performed "Jim Crow" in New York City; Allen Woll, *Black Musical Theatre: From Coontown to Dreamgirls* (Baton Rouge: Louisiana State University Press, 1989) 1.

65. Hildred Roach, *Black American Music: Past and Present* (Boston: Crescendo Publishing Co., 1973) 49.

66. Oscar G. Brockett, *World Drama* (New York: Holt, Rinehart and Winston, Inc., 1984) 319.

67. Garff B. Wilson, *Three Hundred Years of American Drama and Theatre: From Ye Bare and Ye Cubb to Hair* (New Jersey: Prentice-Hall, Inc., 1973) 202.

68. Quoted in Grimsted, 239..

69. Slide, Anthony. *The Vaudevillians: A Dictionary of Vaudeville Performers*, (Connecticut: Arlington House, 1981) xii.

70. Wilson 197-198.

71. James Weldon Johnson, *Black Manhattan* (1930; New York: Arno Press and The New York Times, 1969) 89-90, 95; Mabel M. Smythe, ed., *The Black American Reference Book* (New Jersey: Prentice-Hall, Inc., 1976) 688. Dramatic endeavors with this objective

had begun in 1821 with the African Company at the African Grove Theatre in New York; see *Black Manhattan* 78, and James Hatch, "Some African Influences on the Afro-American Theatre," in Errol Hill, *The Theatre of Black Americans: A Collection of Critical Essays* (1980; New York: Applause Theatre Book Publishers, 1987) 14.

72. A comprehensive source on the history of this genre is Allen Woll, *Black Musical Theatre: From Coontown to Dreamgirls* (Baton Rouge: Louisiana State University Press, 1989).

73. Daphne Duval Harrison, *Black Pearls: Blues Queens of the 1920s* (New Brunswick: Rutgers University Press, 1988) 8.

74. Eileen Southern, *The Music of Black Americans: A History*, 2nd ed. (New York: W.W.Norton and Company, 1983) 242-243; James Weldon Johnson, *Black Manhattan* 98-100; Langston Hughes, "Black Influences in the American Theater: I," Mabel M. Smythe, ed. *The Black American Reference Book* (New Jersey: Prentice-Hall, Inc., 1976) 688.

75. Allen Woll, *Black Musical Theatre: From Coontown to Dreamgirls* (Baton Rouge: Louisiana State University Press, 1989) 7; Hughes "Black Influences," 688; Johnson, *Black Manhattan* 102-103; James Haskins, *Black Dance in America: A History Through It's People* (New York: Harper/Collins Publishers, 1990) 43.

76. Johnson 189.

77. Southern 434.

78. Chris Goddard, "Theater and Dance," *Jazz Away from Home* (New York: Paddington Press, Ltd., 1979) 81; 87. For a comprehensive discussion of the contributions of Blacks to dance in America see Marshall and Jean Stearns, *Jazz Dance* (New York: Macmillan Publishing Co. Inc., 1968).

79. Sandra R. Lieb, *Mother of the Blues: A Study of Ma Rainey* (Massachusetts: The University of Massachusetts Press, 1981) 26-27.

80. Goddard, "Background to the Blues," *Jazz Away from Home* 55.

81. *The Negro Vanguard*, 171; Goddard, "Theater and Dance," *Jazz Away from Home* 83. For comprehensive individual accounts of the lives of these women see Sandra R. Lieb, *Mother of the Blues: A Study of Ma Rainey* (Massachusetts: The University of Massachusetts Press, 1981); Chris Albertson, Bessie (New York: Stein and Day, 1971); Josephine Baker and Jo Bouillon (1977), *Josephine*; Stephen Papich *Remembering Josephine* (1976); and Lynn Haney *Naked at the Feast.*.

82. James Haskins, *Black Theater in America* (New York: Thomas Y. Crowell, 1982) 62-63; Henry T. Sampson, *Blacks in Blackface: A Source Book on early Black Musical Shows* (New Jersey: The Scarecrow Press, Inc., 1980) 14-19; Langston Hughes and Milton Meltzer, *Black Magic: A Pictorial History of Black Entertainers in*

America (New York: Bonanza Books, 1967) 67; Daphne Duval Harrison devotes an entire chapter to the Theatre Owners' Booking Association, "Riding 'Toby' to the Big Time" in *Black Pearls: Blues Queens of the 1920s* (New Brunswick: Rutgers University Press, 1988) 17-41.

83. Robert Kimball and William Bolcom. *Reminiscing with Sissle and Blake*. (New York: The Viking Press, 1973) 148.

84. Kimball, and Bolcom, 100-101.

85. Walter Meserve, "Age of Melodrama: Sensation, Sententia," *The Revels History of Drama in English 1850-1912*, eds, T. W. Craik, Travis Bogard, Richard Moody and Walter J. Meserve (New York: Barnes and Noble Books, 1977) 195.

86. Elsa Honig Fine, *The Afro-American Artist: A Search for Identity* (New York: Holt, Rinehart and Winston, Inc., 1973) 59.

87. Fine 50-51.

88. Fine 63-64; Edgar A. Toppin, *A Biographical History of Blacks in America Since 1528* (New York: David McKay Company, Inc., 1971) 351-352; Elizabeth Hadley Freydberg, "Nineteenth Century Euro-Cultural Influences in the Works of Three Black American Artists," unpublished essay, received the 1984 National Council for Black Studies Scholastic Essay Award. North Carolina, 1984.

89. Fine 68, 71, 67.

90. Southern 350-352.

91. Kimball and Bolcom 86.

92. Al Rose, *Eubie Blake* (New York: Schirmer Books, A Division of Macmillan Publishing Co., Inc., 1979) 57.

93. Rose 57-58; Southern 344-345.

94. Theodore W. Hatlen, *Orientation to the Theater* (New York: Appleton-Century-Crofts, 2nd edition, 1972) 102.

95. *Early Flight: From Balloons to Biplanes*, ed. Frank Oppel (New Jersey: Castle, 1987) 188-196.

96. Geoffrey Perrett, *America in the Twenties: A History* (New York: Simon & Schuster, Inc., 1982) 224.

97. Perrett 227.

98. Enoch P. Waters, personal interview with Elizabeth Hadley Freydberg, and Kathleen Collins 12 January 1985.

99. Elois Coleman Patterson, *Memoirs of the Late Bessie Coleman, Aviatrix* (Elois Patterson, 1969) N. pag.

100. "Aviatrix Must Sign Away Life To Learn," *The Chicago Defender*, 8 October 1921: 2.

101. Letter from Bessie Coleman to Norman Studios, in the Black Film Center Archive, Indiana University, Bloomington. Courtesy of Professor Phyllis R. Klotman, Director. The letter is dated at "Tampa, Fla, 3rd February, 1926."

III

"Jump at the Sun"

She flew over the Royal Palace, encircled the Eifel [sic] Tower, and spanned the English Channel.

Ross D. Brown

Elizabeth (Bessie) Coleman was born in Atlanta, Texas on January 20, 1896 (eighteen months before Amelia Mary Earhart), the twelfth of thirteen children. Her birthdate has often been questioned because it appears in various places as 1892, and 1893. It seems however, that Coleman appropriated her sister Georgia Coleman's birthday whenever expedient to suit her purpose of registering herself as older than she really was. Her mother Susan Coleman, was an African American. Her father, George Coleman, was three quarters Choctaw Indian and one quarter African. While Bessie was still a toddler, the Coleman family moved to Waxahachie, Texas, an agricultural region and trade center that produced cotton, grain and cattle, about thirty miles south of Dallas and recognized as the cotton capital of the West. By the time the Colemans moved there, it had three railroads: the Missouri, Kansas, and Texas, the Burlington Rock Island, and the Southern Pacific; one higher educational institution, Trinity University; and later it added two airports.[1]

The move to Waxahachie presented the Coleman family with greater possibilities to find work. Here, the Coleman family made a living from picking cotton. Mr. Coleman stayed long enough to build a three room house on 1/4 acre of land. But by the time Bessie was seven years old, he had abandoned the household and returned to Choctaw country in Oklahoma. Marion Coleman, Bessie's niece, said that the story repeatedly echoed among family members regarding Mr. Coleman's departure from home was that Susan Coleman chased him back to his Oklahoma reservation because he was lazy and refused to work.[2] After Mr. Coleman's departure, Susan Coleman raised nine children alone as she continued to harvest in the fields, pick cotton, and do domestic work to make ends meet. When the children became old enough, usually about eight years old, they too had to work in the cotton fields to supplement the Coleman family income.

Although Bessie was an obedient child, she opted to eschew the activities of cotton-picking which rendered blood-pricked fingertips, and backaches caused by stooping from sun-up to sun-down, preferring instead to daydream and read. Monetarily, she contributed very little to the household economy because daydreaming hampered her productivity in the fields. Susan Coleman recognized that Bessie was destined for something different in life, so she like Zora Neale Hurston's mother, encouraged Bessie to "jump at the sun—We might not land on the sun, but at least we would get off the ground."[3] She exempted Bessie from working in the cotton fields, but assigned her the responsibility of bookkeeping for the other cotton pickers in the family because of her excellent mathematical skills. Thus when they traveled to town to collect their payment, Bessie went along to insure that they were not cheated by the white people who customarily took advantage of illiterate African American workers.

Susan Coleman nurtured the dreamer and fortified the seeds of curiosity and difference in her exceptional young daughter with a steady supply of books purchased from a wagon library that traveled through their town biannually. It was from these books that the children learned about Booker T. Washington, ex-slave founder of Tuskegee University, read of Harriet Tubman's successes leading three hundred slaves to freedom, and were introduced to literature by African American poet Paul Laurence Dunbar.[4] In addition to acquiring a formal education, Bessie was gaining a sense of her identity as an African American with a heritage to be proud of. Intellectual thought at this time widely denied that African Americans had ever done anything; all great contributions were still somewhere on the horizon. African Americans had no choice but to assimilate because they had no culture distinctive enough to qualify as one. Many African Americans, however, attribute a great deal of their success to early readings along just such lines.

The exchanges between the burgeoning fields of aviation and *belles lettres* were more common than has been acknowledged. For example, Paul Laurence Dunbar, "Negro Poet Laureate," was encouraged on several occasions by the popular American dramatist James A. Herne (1839-1901) to publish. Herne was so delighted he passed Dunbar's work along to literary critic William Dean Howells; and Howells apparently extended the chain by alerting the famous aviation pioneer Orville Wright to Dunbar's potential. Upon receiving such lofty recommendation, Wright printed Dunbar's short-lived African American newspaper, the *Dayton Tattler* (1889).

It is known that Dunbar's work inspired Bessie's *esprit de corps,* as well as her perspective on life; perhaps she had knowledge of the Dunbar-Wright connection. Nevertheless, Dunbar's published works had been distributed nationwide in periodicals as early as 1888, and in published volumes in 1893. Even though she often read aloud from Stowe's *Uncle Tom's Cabin,* her negation of the character during her youth was most probably derived from Dunbar's characterization of Uncle Tom as a traitor to his people, as evidenced in his short story "A Council of State."[5] Dunbar transposed the Uncle Tom character into the characterization of Miss Kirkman, a mulatto who deplores being identified with and maltreated as other African Americans. Miss Kirkman is so despicable in the betrayal of other African Americans that it is conceivable that the impression made on the mind of a young Bessie forced her to spend a lifetime dedicated to expunging the image of *Uncle Tom* and in avoiding becoming an "Uncle Tom."[6] Coleman was exposed to African American nationalism in several of Dunbar's poems, but his "Ode to Ethiopia" is explicit on this topic, in his insistence to

> Be proud, my Race, in mind and soul;
> Thy name is writ on Glory's scroll
>   In characters of fire.
> High 'mid the clouds of Fame's bright sky
> Thy banner's blazoned folds now fly,
>   And truth shall lift them higher.
> . . . .
> Go on and up! Our souls and eyes
> Shall follow the continuous rise;
>   Our ears shall list thy story
> From bards who from thy root shall spring,
> And proudly tune their lyres to sing
>   Of Ethiopia's glory.[7]

Dunbar's poem "Sympathy," rich with imagery of a struggling caged bird fighting to fly free, might have served Bessie as a coping mechanism in its exclamations:

> I know what the caged bird feels, alas!
>   When the sun is bright on the upland slopes;
> When the wind stirs soft through the springing
>   grass,
> And the river flows like a stream of glass;
> When the first bird sings and the first bud

opes,
And the faint perfume from its chalice steals—
I know what the caged bird feels!
I know why the caged bird beats his wing
      Till its blood is red on the cruel bars;
For he must fly back to his perch and cling
When he fain would be on the bough a-swing;
      And a pain still throbs in the old, old scars
And they pulse again with a keener sting—
I know why he beats his wing!
I know why the caged bird sings, ah me,
      When his wing is bruised and his bosom sore,—
When he beats his bars and he would be free;
It is not a carol of joy or glee,
      But a prayer that he sends from his heart's
            deep core,
But a plea, that upward to Heaven he flings—
I know why the caged bird sings![8]

Bessie must have envisioned herself as a caged bird during her childhood days of daydreaming and reading books—activities that were her only connection to a world beyond Waxahachie, Texas and cotton fields; and intuitively knew, "what the caged bird feels!"

Dunbar's works may have further prepared Coleman for the deception of Northern urban life, and the racist structure of white political, social, and cultural institutions designed to maintain the subjugation of African Americans. In many ways, Dunbar's works were a harbinger of the Garveyism she later found so sustaining and compelling. During her lifetime, Coleman even traveled the very avenues that Dunbar did. Both lived in Chicago, had short stints in New York and associated with entertainers; and while Dunbar lived briefly in Jacksonville, Florida, Coleman's life came to end in that city. Although she was undoubtedly impressed with the heroism of Tubman that most likely instilled her with a determination to make a contribution to her race, and with the accomplishments of Washington, Coleman's courage was predictably sustained by literary works of Dunbar and by her mother's love and encouragement.

Susan Coleman could not read until she was about fifty, but when one of her children became old enough, she would excuse that child from picking cotton and harvesting and send him or her to the elementary division of the Colored Agricultural and Normal University in Langston, Oklahoma, with the expectation to learn how to read and return home and teach the younger ones made explicitly. The Coleman home was a religious Baptist home, and each child was expected to demonstrate reading skills by reading aloud from the Bible every evening.[9] Bessie, the daydreamer, developed into an impetuous and voracious reader, who apparently performed or gave impromptu dramatic readings for family members when she felt so inspired by her text. Elois Patterson, Bessie's elder sister, recounting Bessie's dramatic rendition of the reading of *Uncle Tom's Cabin* to family members, wrote that

> sometimes she would brush away a tear, and at times with the sense of humor that she always had, she would laugh, though reluctantly; but she said after finishing the book. 'I'll never be a Topsy or an Uncle Tom.'[10]

It is evident from this description that the young Bessie manifested an early inventiveness, a quick intelligence, and a desire already at this tender age to perform for others— entertaining and stirring emotions of family members with her dramatic renditions. Dramatic renditions of the Bible were further stirred, nourished and intensified by the great emotional reservoirs of the Negro Spirituals, which were an integral part of her childhood home. Susan Coleman, having recognized Bessie's extraordinary intelligence and ambition during her early childhood, enrolled her in school. Whereas she allowed her other children to attend school whenever time and work permitted, she sacrificed Bessie's much needed financial contributions to the family, and registered her on a continuing basis.

Susan Coleman, like the young Sarah Bredlove (Madame C.J. Walker), did laundry at home for white people. As an independent contractor working in her own home, she had more control over working conditions than her sisters living and working in the houses of others, because she could determine when her workday began and when it ended. At the same time, she could maintain some semblance of family life in the rearing and education of her children. Also African American washerwomen in Texas, having recognized their indispensability to white people, had mounted a militant strike for higher wages as early as 1877.[11] When Bessie was old enough to wash and iron for white people, her mother permitted her to save her earnings for her college education.

Bessie's mother enrolled her in the elementary division of the Colored Agricultural and Normal University, popularly known as Langston named for the great uncle of the man who was to become the American Poet Laureate of the twentieth century, Langston Hughes. Langston Hughes was named after his mother's uncle John Mercer Langston, who had distinguished himself as an educator, politician, founder, dean and president of the Howard Law School. The Colored Agricultural and Normal University, located in Langston, Oklahoma housed an elementary division (5-12), a high school, and a Teacher's College. Student enrollment represented twenty Oklahoma territorial counties, as well as Texas and Missouri.[12] The earliest extant official records of Elizabeth Coleman's enrollment is dated 1911, and indicate that she was in the sixth grade (school records were destroyed by fire in 1907). Coleman entered the High School where she had to pass four years of English, two years of mathematics, one year of American history or civics, and sixteen credits of languages, in order to graduate and be admitted to the Teacher's College.[13] After graduating from High School, Coleman attended the Teacher's College for one year, where all students were required to study English, algebra, Latin, physiology, and botany during their first year.[14] According to Marion Coleman, although she achieved excellence in this course of study, Bessie's education was curtailed after one year in attendance when her finances were depleted. According to her sister Elois, Bessie was so popular with the other students, that she was accompanied home by members of the School band upon her withdrawal from the University.[15]

Coleman's return to Waxahachie was brief, because shortly after her return she, like so many other African Americans of the period, migrated to Chicago where two of her brothers lived. As noted in the previous chapter, her decision was personal, but was framed by a national phenomenon. Bessie Coleman migrated in order to find desirable employment, between 1915 and 1917. Although the exact date of her migration is unknown, it is known that by 1917, she had earned enough money to move her mother and sisters to Chicago.[16] Her older brother, Walter was a Pullman porter. During the late nineteenth and early twentieth centuries, Pullman porters, predominantly African American in ranks, were the new class of "professionals," and were held in high regard by the rest of the community. They were, after all, well-paid. They were also the carriers of the *The Chicago Defender*, that embodied the hopes and dreams of the North for the people in the South—an impetus in the great migration. They were the ambassadors of the rising Black bourgeoisie that finally saw itself as the first generation of a Talented Tenth as defined by W. E. B. Du Bois.

After Coleman arrived in Chicago, she moved in with her younger brother, Johnny, a veteran of World War I and a cook for Al Capone, the notorious racketeer. Upon his return from France, he, like all African Americans who had fought the war for democracy, found that democracy was not extended to them in the "land of the free, and the home of the brave"—the United States of America—his homeland. Instead of finding employment upon their return, they found rampant racism, race riots and brutality meted out to them by law abiding white American citizens. Some white Americans who were not law abiding such as Al Capone, however, employed African Americans as cooks, waiters, and musicians in their homes, nightclubs and speakeasies.

Capone and other gangsters of the time had their own agenda that circumvented federal law. While they were primarily interested in sidestepping prohibition laws, in order to profit from liquor sales, they relaxed the Jim Crow practices that mandated separation of Blacks and whites, when it was in their interest to do so. Langston Hughes's comments about the Cotton Club in New York suggest such profitable exceptions to the rule. Although Black performers were the primary entertainment at the Cotton Club, any African American without a superstar's name was not permitted to fraternize with the white clientele. As Hughes describes it, the Cotton Club "was a Jim Crow club for gangsters and moneyed whites. They were not cordial to Negroes except celebrities like Bojangles."[17] But Hughes's statement of disgust does reveal that exceptions were made for Black celebrities like Bill "Bojangles" Robinson.

Combined with commentary on the extent these diverse elements of the community mixed, Earl "Father" Hines, pianist *extrodinaire* who developed the trumpet style piano playing, also presents an image of Al Capone that is in direct contrast to his popularized media image. According to Hines, Capone had a humanitarian side which fostered his popularity among black and poor people; he provided free meals for the hungry, housing for the homeless, employment in his nightclubs and restaurants, and extended generous gratuities to many black nightclub performers. In this environment where diverse elements of people mingled after hours, "you didn't know what you were, a musician, a show person or a gangster. Everybody was mixing, having a great time."[18]

From this description it is understandable why Johnny Coleman spent the remainder of his life employed by Capone. Just as Bessie Coleman had avoided the back-breaking work of cotton-picking in Texas, she also eschewed conventional women's labor in Chicago—she sought neither domestic, nor factory work, the prevalent occupations for African American women migrants of the day. Instead, she like Madame C. J. Walker sought alternative employment in Beauty Culture. Coleman took manicuring classes at the Burnham's School of Beauty Culture and in a short time obtained a job as a manicurist in the White Sox Barbershop, where her clientele were "men of the streets" and "the underworld—men who had the time and the luxury to care for their fingernails."[19] The barber shop was located on 35th Street on Southside Chicago (comparable to 125th Street in Harlem) within a sixteen block strip that housed the Grand Theatre, the Savoy Ballroom, the Binga State Bank and offices of *The Chicago Defender*. It was the avenue of both business and pleasure for African Americans, who also owned or operated many of the restaurants, barbershops, haberdasheries, clubs and theatres in this neighborhood that sparkled after dark "like Paris," and was populated by the "most dangerous people in the world."[20]

The primary clientele of the barbershops, the clubs, and the cabarets were racketeers, entertainers, businessmen, and pimps. The barbershop was where men of this ilk initiated and consummated business deals. Racketeers were synonymous with cabarets and nightclubs during this era, when the federal government was enforcing the Volstead Act (1920-33). They fermented the bootleg liquor in basements and marketed it in the night spots, which surely activated the "roar" in the twenties. Racketeers, entertainers, businessmen, and pimps depended on their appearance to enhance their authority with the customers. The barbershops and the haberdasheries profited from this concern.

While the men frequented the barbershops and clubs to make contacts, business exchanges, and to advance backroom gambling, the women could be found in the cabarets and clubs as headliners, chorus girls, waitresses, and prostitutes waiting to surrender their earnings to their pimps before continuing their stroll. Lil Hardin (1902-1974), jazz pianist, composer and conductor, played the Dreamland, the Royal Gardens and the Pekin Theatre during these years that Bessie Coleman frequented these establishments. It was Hardin who hired the young Louis Armstrong to play coronet for her and eventually encouraged him to strike out as a soloist.[21] In the same time frame, a young Alberta Hunter was the headliner at the Dreamland.

City life after hours with its nightclubs, cabarets, and speakeasies was like a fantastic amusement park for many of the southern migrants who began to seek refuge from the cramped living styles and from the drudgery of their daily work. They were like children left unattended in a candy store. Coleman was no different; she too gallivanted around Southside Chicago seeking amusement after working hours with running buddies Alberta Hunter, Josephine Baker, Ethel Waters, and the king of tap dancers, Bill "Bojangles" Robinson.[22] Waters had already been to Europe by the time they met, and Baker was to go to Paris in 1925 with the cast of *La Revue Nègre*, where within a year she had become a star at the *Folies Bergère*.

Equality was a peculiar by-product borne of the illegal activities during the prohibition years. Whereas previously women were excluded from lounges, pubs, saloons, and taverns, exclusively male establishments, with prohibition they were permitted to "bend elbows with the boys." Women in a variety of capacities populated the nightclubs, cabarets, and the speakeasies. Regarding the atmosphere of speakeasies during the twenties, Geoffrey Perrett states that

> all of the customers, men and women alike, were breaking the law together. That they were owned by gangsters seemed to trouble no one. Nor did the presence of B-girls and drunk-rollers, or the outbreak of shootings and stabbings when the

gangsters started making war on each other. There was overcharging on a prodigious scale. Yet nothing seemed to keep the customers from coming back for more. For various reasons, a great many Americans evidently enjoyed Prohibition, so long as they could buy a drink.[23]

This statement can be expanded to include the nightclubs and cabarets.[24] Chicago boasted some of the best nightclubs featuring the giants of blues and jazz music who sauntered in from New Orleans after the government closed down the cat houses and the honky-tonks in the red light districts during the war. Lil Hardin, jazz pianist, composer and conductor (later the wife of Louis Armstrong), Bessie Smith, empress of the blues, Alberta Hunter, vocalist and musical stage actress, a teenaged Josephine Baker, not yet "La Bakir," and Ethel Waters whose career encompassed many genres, were all Coleman's contemporaries, playing the clubs and the rent parties. Bessie Coleman hung out after hours with these entertainers, frequently after Alberta Hunter the headliner during these years, had performed at the Dreamland, located in the same district and on the same street as the barbershop where Coleman worked. All of these women were in their youth and enjoyed carousing when they were not working.

The Dreamland was the most exclusive club in Chicago for excellent music, floor shows, great dancing, and an all-around good time, and was a favorite haunting place of these women. Some of the male performers were Coleman's barbershop customers. Many Chicagoans still maintain today that during this era if entertainers did not play the Dreamland, they would never play the prestigious Cotton Club in New York.[25] When performers like Earl "Father" Hines, Louis Armstrong, Jelly Roll Morton, and King Oliver were not at the clubs, they could be found at house rent parties—parties held to raise money for people having difficulty meeting their rent payments; and at after hours clubs—unlicensed clubs that opened after the licensed clubs had closed. There the music was just as good, and sometimes far superior, because musicians from several of the Chicago clubs gathered at these parties and jammed all night long.

It was in the masculine environment of her workplace that Coleman listened to men who had returned from World War I, including her brother Johnny, discuss the war and the fledgling field of aviation. Coleman's brother, Johnny used to hang out at the barbershop where she worked and tease her about women who flew planes in France.[26] Discussion concerning the infant field of aviation was prevalent in the male conversations of the day. Carl Sandburg characterized the ethos of the Black Belt of Chicago in 1919 as an atmosphere permeated with patriotism that was proudly exhibited in window displays of barber shops, smoke shops, and men's clothing stores. It was comprised of photographs, wartime paraphernalia, and personal items from African American regiments that had fought the war in France.[27]

Coleman developed an intense interest in aviation and began to study extended weekly reports of the daring exploits of African American pilots and soldiers. These articles appeared in the *Chicago Defender* and in the more conservative *Chicago Whip*, and were often accompanied by photographs, especially those of the segregated New York 15th and Illinois 8th regiments—the first and second African American regiments shipped to France in World War I. They also reported stories of homogeneous treatment of African Americans in France. The atmosphere of Coleman's workplace, coupled with newspaper reports, served to enhance her desire to pursue aviation, and also made her dream appear attainable.

Coleman's passion for aviation finally dominated her course of action. Leaving her sister Georgia as her replacement, Coleman quit her job as manicurist at the White Sox Barbershop, and focused her attention on becoming an aviator.[28] Coleman queried aviation schools in the Chicago area to determine tuition expenses. During these initial interviews she first learned that she would not be admitted because of her race and gender. Each time she located a school, she was told that she would not be admitted because she was an African American and a woman. "Flight schools here [United States] had white instructors and white students. There were only about a dozen licensed women pilots then [1920], and most of them had gone abroad for flight lessons."[29] Although the Aero Club of Illinois had been established in 1910, the Chicago School of Aviation in 1911, and by 1912 neophyte aviators were traveling nationwide to study aviation at The Cicero Field Flight School in Illinois, these runways were closed to Bessie Coleman. Coleman refused to be dissuaded, and escalated her determination to achieve her dream.

Although Coleman more than likely received generous gratuities from customers at the barber shop, she knew that her income and savings earned from manicuring were insufficient to meet the tuition costs of an aviation school, so she started her own business to increase her income. Coleman established a chili parlor at Thirty-Fifth and Indiana Avenue, one block from the offices of the *Chicago Defender*. She then opened a savings account at the Binga State Bank. Both Robert Abbott, founder and editor of the *Chicago Defender*, and Jesse Binga, founder of the Binga State Bank, African American philanthropists, were later to become instrumental in Coleman's trip to France.[30] When Coleman had accrued what she thought to be a sufficient sum for her education in aviation, she turned to Robert Abbott for advice on how to achieve her objective.

Robert Abbott (1870-1940), the son of former slaves, and an attorney, was to become one of the first African American millionaires through revolutionizing the African American press. Abbott was highly respected by African Americans as a man who walked the streets with the common folk in his Chicago community, always displaying interest in others. He had become renowned and quite influential in African American communities nationally for expressing concern for African Americans throughout the United States in his weekly *Chicago Defender*. He used the *Chicago Defender* to speak out against racism and lynchings, and to encourage Northern migration, racial unity, and African American uplift through education and self-help.

Indeed, it is his printed words in the *Chicago Defender* that are credited by many as being one of the primary forces in orchestrating the swell in numbers of the great Northern migration. His influence was considered so great, that some Southern communities enacted laws making it illegal for African Americans to purchase or read the *Chicago Defender*—breaking this law was punishable by imprisonment, compulsory farm labor, lashings and other means.[31] In addition to hand carrying copies of the newspapers to barber shops, poolrooms, drugstores, churches and peoples' homes, Abbott enlisted African American railway porters (Walter Coleman, Bessie's elder brother was one), entertainers, and others whose professions involved travel, to circulate the *Chicago Defender* from North to South. The reason for this unusual mode of distribution was not only financial. In the deep South, even the United States postmasters could not be trusted to deliver what some whites believed to be a subversive publication safely.

The first issue of the *Chicago Defender:* "The Worlds Greatest Weekly" materialized on May 5, 1905, the same year of the first meeting of the Niagara Movement, the precursor of the N.A.A.C.P. Robert Abbott, who as a young man set type for Ferdinand Barnett, editor of the *Conservator* (Ida B. Wells-Barnett's husband), directed his messages to the African American masses which lent to the popularity of his circulation.

> He [Abbott] cultivated a homey, direct style of expression, never "talking down" to his readers, and demanded that his writers follow this policy. The paper became the "bible" and inspiration of black Southerners yearning toward the New Canaan, and the "defender" indeed of those already in the North.[32]

The literary organs of the N.A.A.C.P. and National Urban League, in contrast, were directed at the African American elite. The *Chicago Defender's* adversary newspapers "had attached themselves to one or the

other of the dominant political parties (usually the Republican), and too
often had subordinated the battle for justice and equality to political
expediency."[33] African Americans in Chicago knew that Abbott
maintained an open-door policy; anyone could go to him with a
problem and he would make an effort to help resolve it.

Coleman went through that opened door and was advised by Abbott
to learn French; because, he said, "if you do not speak the language of a
country you are almost as good as deaf and dumb."[34] He advised her to
go to France where Baroness de la Roche and Hélène Dutrieu had already
received distinction for their aeronautic accomplishments. Baroness de la
Roche was acclaimed as the first licensed aviatrix, having received her
license in 1910; by 1913 Dutrieu had received recognition both in
France and the United States for establishing long distance records for
French women.[35] To be sure, American women such as Blanche Scott
had begun flying in 1910. Harriet Quimby in 1911, Matilde Moisant in
1911, Ruth Law in 1912, Katherine and Marjorie Stinson in 1912 and
1914, and Amelia Earhart in 1921, were publicly flying airplanes in the
United States at this time. They were white however, usually
upperclass, and were permitted to purchase their own private planes.
These women, contemporaries of Coleman's, also experienced rejection
from aviation schools; but Harriet Quimby and Matilde Moisant were
good friends. John Moisant, Matilde's brother, had established his own
flying school, the Moisant International Aviators, where Harriet and
Matilde learned to fly.[36] Scott was trained by Glenn Curtiss who
disapproved of women flying;[37] and Law's husband purchased her first
plane and she learned to fly in Boston.[38] Katherine and Majorie Stinson
were trained at the Wright School in Dayton and in Chicago at the
Cicero Field, and were licensed by the Aero Club of Illinois. Later their
mother established the Stinson School of Flying (1915) in San
Antonio, Texas where they taught Canadian males.[39] Several months
after Amelia Earhart declared that she wanted to fly, her mother helped
her purchase a $2,000 sportsplane and she immediately undertook
aviation training with woman instructor, Neta Snook, at Los Angeles'
Rogers Airport.[40] Coleman was also fortunate enough to have a mother
who nurtured and encouraged her desires, but her mother was a
washerwoman, who did not have $2,000 to purchase an airplane, nor to
provide the cost of tuition for her daughter to attend an aviation
institution.[41]

Coleman followed Abbott's advice and studied French at a Berlitz
school located in the Chicago Loop. Upon completion of her language
requirements, she withdrew her savings from the Binga State Bank in
preparation for her departure to France. Coleman also met with Jesse
Binga and secured additional financial backing from him for her trip
abroad. With his financial support and that of Abbott, Coleman sailed
to Du Crotoy Somme, France in November 1920.

Binga and Abbott, then, were the benefactors behind the practical business spirit that established African American priorities in Chicago during the early 1920s. The better recognized Renaissance in Harlem focused on racial uplift through artistic and, by the broadest and kindest measure, humanistic endeavors. While Harlem-centered activities had some nominal impact on the national African American community, they were directed at the Talented Tenth, an elite group circumscribed and ultimately limited by its own class prejudices.

Chicago-style racial uplift, which took care of business endeavors first, had consequences which reached farther than its immediate beneficiaries. In the balance, the business orientation in Chicago calling for "racial self-reliance"[42] far outlasted the results of arts-based efforts of Harlem. The emphasis on economic self-sufficiency as a base for equality recognized that white patronage and paternalistic interests were bound to falter. And falter they did, with the onslaught of the Great Depression. The New Negro, when identified solely with Art, was merely superfluous. Indeed, erstwhile Chicago millionaires and industry magnates, such as George Pullman, P. D. Armour, Gustavas Swift and Potter Palmer, could no longer afford to be entertained or amused—or at least not to pay for their amusement so lavishly.

Both Abbott and Binga, cognizant of their location in Chicago, promoted self-reliance in their business lives as well as their behaviors as private citizens. Robert Abbott agitated locally for employment, housing and political inclusion of African American masses. Jesse Binga fought vigorously for the economic welfare of the African American community too. He provided property and housing through his real estate office, and loans for the establishment of community businesses through his bank. Both men believed in returning benefits to the communities which had nourished them, and in increasing the magnitude of the benefits they had received, if possible. For both men, that was possible.

It would be inaccurate, of course, to assert flatly that the various African American cultural and political organizations or exponents diverged completely in their focus. Far from it. All had one common denominator: they were all nationalistic, claiming a long and proud heritage and racial identity as their own. All fought for the racial uplift of African Americans. Only the routes to that goal diverged.

Bessie Coleman, though reared in Texas, revealed herself a true daughter of Chicago in her ambitions. She was restless, soon tiring of manicuring and living vicariously through the aviation stories narrated by barbershop customers. Coleman socialized with artists and entertainers, but she had no intentions of falling into step with the hardships and sufferings of her sisters in entertainment on the T. O. B. A. circuit. At least two sources indicate that Coleman traveled with this circuit,[43] but it seems that she had no desire of becoming just another hungry chorine, in a stage and cabaret industry glutted with women.

Her single most distinguishing feature was her insistence that she be independent—like her mother before her, who was her own manager as an independent laundress. In fact, she was not above straying from the path established by her mentors. Abbott, for example, was a violent Garvey adversary. The antipathy is in some ways a surprising one, since both men were staunchly devoted to uplifting the status of African Americans. But Abbott was a highly-educated and meticulous businessman, while Garvey appealed to the proletariat masses. Moreover, the Harlem-Chicago intellectual schism was no doubt a factor in Abbott's dislike of Garveyism. Harlem intellectuals stressed the production of distinctively Black art and other cultural forms, while Chicago thinkers believed that economic parity was the most important first goal for African Americans. Still, notwithstanding Abbott's dislike of Garvey and his following, Coleman, Abbott's protégé, counted among her friends, and even among her beaux, a number of Garveyites. Reverend Junius Caesar Austin (1887-1968), political activist, friend and supporter of Coleman and founder "of the first organizations of Negro aviators in the United States in May 1935 at Pilgrim Baptist Church."[44] Austin, like Coleman, was affiliated with and active in both Garvey's U.N.I.A. organization and the N.A.A.C.P. Prince Kojo Tovalou-Houenou (1887-1936), one of the high potentates in the U.N.I.A. was one of her beaux.[45]

Her independence was guided by the steady hand of pragmatism. She chose to concentrate on the business of learning to fly and eventually establishing an aviation school when she realized the seriousness of her calling to fly. She was also guided by the Chicago nationalistic influence: that one's personal endeavors should be an asset to the entire race, rather than the fortunate few.

During the latter part of 1920, Coleman received an acceptance letter from the Condrau School of Aviation in Du Crotoy, France written in French which she could now read. Her passport application , dated November 9, 1920, witnessed by a friend Anna M. Tyson, and her brother, John Coleman all residents of 4533 Indiana Avenue, Chicago Illinois; states that Bessie Coleman was going abroad to study in England, France and Italy.[46] At twenty-four years of age Bessie Coleman was finally on the "runway" bound for France in pursuit of her dream of becoming an aviator.

Notes

1. Helen Goodlett, "Waxahachi, Texas," *The Handbook of Texas*, ed. Walter Prescott Welch, vol. II (Austin: The Texas State Historical Association, 1952) 871-72.

2. Marion Coleman, personal interview with Elizabeth Hadley Freydberg and Kathleen Collins, 12 January 1985.

3. Zora Neale Hurston, a prolific writer during the Harlem Renaissance and Coleman's contemporary. Hurston's mother urged her daughter to "'jump at de sun.' We might not land on the sun, but at least we would get off the ground." Quoted by Robert E. Hemenway *Zora Neale Hurston: A Literary Biography*, foreword by Alice Walker, (Chicago: University of Illinois Press, 1977) 14.

4. Elois Coleman Patterson, *Memoirs of the Late Bessie Coleman Aviatrix: Pioneer of the Negro People in Aviation* (Elois Coleman Patterson, 1969) N. pag.

5. All references to this work are taken from Paul Laurence Dunbar, *The Strength of Gideon and Other Stories* (1899; New York: Dodd Mead & Company, 1900) 315-338.

6. Elois Coleman Patterson, N. pag.; "Texas Negro Girl Becomes Able Aviatrix," *Houston Post Dispatch* 7 May 1925: 4.

7. *The Complete Poems of Paul Laurence Dunbar*, with an introduction to "Lyrics of Lowly Life" by W. D. Howells (1895; New York: Dodd, Mead and Company, 1913) 15-16.

8. *The Complete Poems of Paul Laurence Dunbar*, 102.

9 Elois Coleman Patterson, N. pag.

10. Elois Coleman Patterson, N. pag.

11. Dorothy Sterling, "Washerwomen, Maumas, Exodusters, Jubileers," *We Are Your Sisters: Black Women in the Nineteenth Century* (New York: W. W. Norton and Company, 1984) 356-357.

12. Zella J. Black Patterson, *Langston University: A History* (Oklahoma: University of Oklahoma Press, Norman, Publishing Division of the University, 1979) 110. For a comprehensive account of the life of John Mercer Langston see William and Aimee Lee Cheek, *John Mercer Langston and the Fight for Black Freedom 1829-65* (Chicago: University of Illinois Press, 1989).

13. Zella J. Black Patterson 76.

14. Zella J. Black Patterson 76.

15. Elois Coleman Patterson N. pag.

16. Elois Coleman Patterson N. pag.; and Marion Coleman Interview.

17. Langston Hughes, "When Harlem Was In Vogue," *Town & Country*, July 1940: 49.

18. Stanley Dance, *The World of Earl Hines* (New York: Da Capo Press, Inc., 1977) 61.

19Marion Coleman, personal interview.

20. Dance 47.

21. Sally Placksin, "Lil Hardin Armstrong," *American Women in Jazz: 1900 to the Present Their Words, Lives, and Music* (New York: Wideview Books/A Division of PEI Books, Inc., 1982) 60.

22. Marion Coleman, personal interview.

23. Geoffrey Perrett, *America in the Twenties: A History* (New York: Simon and Schuster, Inc., 1982) 177.

24. There are a plethora of personal accounts by African American entertainers with descriptions on what it was like to work in these places--most notably, Stanley Dance, *The World of Earl Hines* (New York: Da Capo Press, Inc., 1977); Jim Haskins, *The Cotton Club* (London: Robson Books, 1985); Ethel Waters, with Charles Samuels, *His Eye Is on the Sparrow* (New York, 1978); Cab Calloway and Bryant Rollins, *Of Minnie the Moocher and Me* (New York: Thomas Crowell Company, 1976); Sally Placksin, "Alberta Hunter," *American Women in Jazz: 1900 to the Present Their Words, Lives, and Music*, (New York: Wideview Books/A Division of PEI Books, Inc., 1982) 36-39.

25. Marion Coleman, personal interview; and Enoch P. Waters, personal interview with Elizabeth Hadley Freydberg and Kathleen Collins, 12 January 1985.

26. Elois Coleman Patterson N. pag.; and Marion Coleman personal interview.

27. Carl Sandburg, *The Chicago Race Riots: July, 1919*, preface by Ralph McGill, intro. Walter Lippmann (1919, 1947, New York: Harcourt, Brace & World, Inc., 1969) 8. Also, Richard Wright captures this ethos regarding aviation and Jim Crow in Chicago in his renowned *Native Son* (1940), set in Black Belt Chicago ca. 1919. The stage adaptation (1941) by Richard Wright and Paul Green retained the following excerpt taken from the novel. As the protagonist, Bigger and his friends watch with "childlike wonder" an airplane sky-writing, the following exchange takes place between them. "'I *could* fly a plane if I had a chance,' Bigger said. 'If you wasn't black and if you had some money and if they'd let you go to that aviation school, you could fly a plane,' Gus said.'" *Native Son* (New York: Harper & Brothers Publishers, 1940) 14.

28. Marion Coleman, personal interview. Note: Georgia was Marion Coleman's mother, and Bessie Coleman's sister.

29. Marjorie Kriz, "Bessie Coleman, Aviation Pioneer," *U. S. Department of Transportation News* (U. S. Department of

Transportation Federal Aviation Administration Office of Public Affairs, Great Lakes Region, n.d.) 1.

30. For a comprehensive account of Abbott's life see Roi Ottley, *The Lonely Warrior: The Life and Times of Robert S. Abbott* (Chicago: Henry Regnery Company, 1955).

31. Arna Bontemps and Jack Conroy, *Anyplace But Here* (1945, Originally published as *They Seek a City*; New York: Hill and Wang, 1966) 158-159.

32. Bontemps and Conroy 106.

33. Bontemps and Conroy 105.

34. Roi Ottley, *The Lonely Warrior: The Life and Times of Robert S. Abbott* (Chicago: Henry Regnery Company, 1955) 269.

35. Charles E. Planck, *Women with Wings* (New York: Harper & Brothers Publishers, 1942) 15-16.

36. Judy Lomax, "The Good Old Crazy Days in America," *Women of the Air* (New York: Dodd, Mead and Company, 1987) 24.

37. Lomax 27.

. Sherwood Harris, *The First to Fly: Aviations's Pioneer Days* (New York: Simon and Schuster, 1970) 254.

39. Roger Bilstein and Jay Miller, "Men, Myths, and Machines: Early Civil Aviation and Its Legacy," *Aviation in Texas* (Texas: Texas Monthly Press, 1985) 14; David Young and Neal Callahan, *Fill the Heavens With Commerce: Chicago Aviation 1855-1926* (Chicago: Chicago Review Press, 1981) 138f.

40. Judy Lomax 69.

41. Ann Hodgman and Rudy Djabbaroff, *Sky-Stars: The History of Women in Aviation.* (New York: Atheneum, 1981) 35.

42. Ottley, *Lonely Warrior* 82.

43. Henry T. Sampson, *Blacks in Blackface: A Source Book on Early Black Musical Shows.* (New Jersey: The Scarecrow Press, Inc., 1980).

44. Randall K. Burkett. "The Baptist Church in the Years of Crisis: J.C. Austin and Pilgrim Baptist Church, 1926-50." Unpublished essay, presented at a joint session of the American Society of Church History and the American Historical Association, the Northeast Seminar on Black Religion, and Religion and Society Series, University of Utah. By permission of Randall K. Burkett, W.E.B. DuBois Institute for Afro-American Research, Harvard University, c. 1991.

45. Elois Coleman Patterson, N. pag. Information on Kojos' affiliation with the U.N.I.A. appears in Patrick Manning and James S. Speigler, "Kojo Tovalou-Houenou: Franco-Dahomean Patriot." Unpublished essay, presented at the African Studies Association. Chicago, November 1988. By permission of Patrick Mannning,

Departments of African American Studies and History, Northeastern
University/Boston.

46. Record Group 59, General Records of the Department of State,
Passport Applications. National Archives and Records Administration:
Washington, DC.

IV

"Lady Didn't Your Plane Stop Up There?"

She believed in service rather than sentiment, she loved performance better than pleasure, she gave exhibitions and not excuses. She pushed her silver wings thru [sic] the clefts of the lazy clouds and brought back a wonderful story of the stars.

Ross D. Brown

After Coleman arrived in Somme Crotcy, France to begin classes, her instructors attempted to discourage her from training. They had reversed their decision to accept women as students after two women had recently fallen to their deaths. She refused to give up her dream, however, so they had her sign a contract relieving the school of all risk and responsibility for her life. During her first week of classes Coleman witnessed the fatal plane crash of a classmate on which she commented that the crash "was a terrible shock to my nerves, but I never lost them, I kept on going."[1]

Coleman found the physical locale of her studies both a challenge and an inspiration. She had to use her limited resources frugally, so she walked nine miles to school every day for ten months.[2] She began to accept these walks as a necessary part of her fitness regiment, since she believed that physical fitness was imperative in the development of a sound and alert mind which was indispensable to a pilot.[3] She was also aware that Somme Crotcy was located near Rouen. There the legendary Joan of Arc (1412-1431) had led French armies against Britain to successfully gain France's freedom, and was imprisoned in a tower, accused by the English of heresy and witchcraft c. 1430-1431.

Coleman later exploited this connection by equating her plight in the United States with that of Joan of Arc in British-occupied France.[4] After completing the ten month course requirements and passing her exams at the Condrau School of Aviation, Coleman continued to study in Paris with an "'ace' who had shot down thirty-one German planes during the World War"[5] to further perfect her newly acquired skills in

81

preparation for the international license exam administered by the Fèdèration Aèronitique Internationale (FAI).

The Fèdèration Aèronitique Internationale was the official organization that mandated the first air safety guidelines in 1910 for France, the United States and sixteen member nations. It continues today to govern the eligibility guidelines for acquisition of an international aviation license, and validate flying records. Because of the proliferation of pilots, as well as surplus WW I aircraft, and homemade airplanes in the early 1920s, this organization could not realistically monitor nor restrict the flight of unlicensed pilots, or supervise the manufacture of safe aircraft. But it could prevent them from participating in authorized air shows and competitive events. Federal regulations for the manufacture of American aircraft and licensing of pilots began in 1926, the year of Coleman's death, with the Air Commerce Act.

For Coleman to be declared a qualified aviator by the FAI, she had to pass a stringent examination that demonstrated several levels of skill comprised of basic life-saving maneuvers

> including twice flying a five-kilometer closed circuit, climbing to a minimum altitude of fifty meters, successfully negotiating a figure eight, landing within fifty meters of a predesignated point, and turning off the engine before touching down.[6]

Bessie Coleman received her international pilot's license No. 18.310, the first awarded to any American woman on June 15, 1921 from the Fèdèration Aèronitique Internationale. Her achievement came eighteen years after the officially recorded historical flight of the airplane by Orville and Wilbur Wright.

During her free time in Paris, Coleman visited aircraft manufacturers and factories to examine airplanes. She observed everything and noted that "flying is as popular in Europe as automobiling is in America."[7] Before Coleman departed France for the United States, she made arrangements to have a 130 horse-power Neuport de Chasse manufactured, to be sent to her in the United States upon its completion. She had decided upon this model for prospective exhibition flights, after having flown several models during her supplemental education in Paris.

The twenty-five-year-old Coleman arrived in New York City on the oceanliner the Manchuria on Sunday, September 29, 1921. When the steamer docked, she was cheerfully greeted by reporters from several national African American periodicals. But the most poignant moment for Bessie Coleman had to have occurred when she gazed beyond the reporters to see the the cast of *Shuffle Along*, that now included her former entertainment companion from Chicago, Josephine Baker. The cast presented Coleman with a silver loving cup to commemorate her achievement.[8] While the gesture was a measure of respect and admiration, it was also one of compassion and recognition of the odds she had faced. They too had to surmount their segregated professional status to arrive on Broadway, the Great White Way, in 1921. Before checking into the Pennsylvania Hotel (later the Statler), Coleman indicated to the press that she intended to inspire African Americans with a desire to fly by performing exhibition flights.[9]

Immediately upon her return to the United States, Coleman set out to find employment in commercial aviation to raise money, to pay for her awaited airplane from Paris, and to begin her exhibition flights. But her triumph soon became bittersweet as she once again experienced rejection because of her race and gender. She was unable to find a suitable job. Continual rejection only strengthened her determination to teach other African Americans to fly. Since there was still a surplus of airplanes available for as little as three hundred to six hundred dollars within the United States, Coleman tenaciously made several attempts to purchase one so that she could more quickly begin her flight business, instead of having to wait for the plane from France. However, she was also denied the right to purchase a plane for the same reasons--she was an African American woman living in the United States in 1921.[10] Although there were no formal laws regulating civilian pilots or the purchase of airplanes, white people guided by a federal government that sanctioned segregation could and did arbitrarily exercise their own racial prejudices in denying Coleman employment both in commercial aviation and in her option to purchase a private plane.

In May 1922, after having exhausted her alternatives at gaining employment and trying to purchase an airplane in the United States, Coleman once again boarded an oceanliner to France to gain additional piloting experience. Although disheartened, she was nowhere near ready to give up. Like so many of her African American sisters and brothers in entertainment, literature, and fine arts, she sought refuge and recognition in France, the country that had established a precedent for congenial reception of African American artists.

A tenacious Coleman hit Europe like a whirlwind this time. In less than seven months, she acquired advanced aviation training in France, Germany, Holland and Switzerland. For the most part, she received on-the-job-training. Coleman studied with Captain Keller, the famous German ace whose reputation was built during World War I aerial dogfights against French and American pilots. She augmented her knowledge of aviation and aircraft by test-piloting airplanes in the Netherlands for Anthony Fokker, the "Flying Dutchman," an accomplished aerobatic stuntman. Fokker was also a renowned aircraft engineer, having designed the Fokker Eindecker (E-III) fighter, one of the most popular fighter planes of World War I because of its propeller-synchronized machine-gun.[11] In her effort to develop her skills as a stuntflyer, she further perfected the basic life-saving maneuvers that she learned during her initial training, into finely polished aerobatic stunts--figure eights, loop-the-loops, trick climbs, and landing a plane with the engine off. Pilots were trained to land a plane with the engine off in preparation for emergency landings in the event of engine failure, fuel shortage, wing damage, and other unexpected hazards.[12] This maneuver was a popular stunt among barnstormers because it intensified audience suspense.[13] At the same time that she studied with accomplished aviators and perfected her skills, Coleman also excited admiration from local news reporters. Although some of the aircraft she piloted were so large, that her activities were considered unladylike, she received continual praise for her display of grace, charm and ease that were to become the hallmarks of her performing persona.

In Stakken, outside of Berlin, Coleman piloted a 220-horsepower Benz motored I. F. G. plane for Pathé News photographers, making it possible for them to photograph the Kaiser's palace from the air. She was hailed by the German newspapers and aviators for flying this airplane without instruction because it was awkward and the largest plane ever flown by a woman at that time. At Friedrichshafen she also exhibited her prowess by test-piloting a Dornier seaplane for the newly founded Dornier Manufactures of large flying boats.[14] The DO-X was one of the earliest aircraft designed for commercial passenger service by Dr. Claude Dornier and was designated by some as the "flying palace," because it housed a recreation room, bathroom, kitchen, and dinette, was designed to seat at least seventy-two people, and was propelled by twelve engines that delivered the 6000 horsepower necessary to lift the 52 tons of weight off the water in 50 seconds and propel it at a velocity of 134 mph.[15] Coleman received high acclaim in the German newspaper for displaying exceptional aeronautical skill in maneuvering this formidable diesel-powered aircraft. After having polished numerous stunt skills, while flying a variety of large and small aircraft, Coleman returned to the United States to begin barnstorming.

Coleman returned equipped with newspaper reportage on her work, letters from famous European flyers attesting to her ability as a superior aviatrix, and newsreels. The newsreels provided especially compelling evidence in the form of celluloid verification. Reporters and letter writers, after all, could be conned into inflated testimony; the camera, at least in these early days of movie-making, could not. She arrived in New York aboard the Noordam from Amsterdam, Holland, on Sunday, August 14, 1922. Among her possessions were credentials from the Aéro Club of France, a letter from the Deutsche Luftreederei (German Aero Club) signed by Captain Keller, a famous German ace, and newspaper articles that included accounts of foreign royalty entertaining her, and Fokker praising her at a banquet as the only American aviator who ever crossed the Kaiser's palace at Potsdam.[16] This time upon her return to the United States, in addition to the ever-present African American reporters, she was greeted by those from *The New York Times* and the *Chicago Tribune*. It was atypical in the 1920s for a white press to report on any but most spectacular activities of African Americans. Therefore, coverage by these prestigious presses is indicative of Coleman's growing international prominence. Under a headline entitled "Negro Aviatrix Arrives," *The New York Times* reported the day after her return that "Bessie Coleman Flew Planes of Many Types in Europe," and that she was designated by "leading French and Dutch aviators as one of the best flyers they had seen."[17]

Coleman pursued her objective with alacrity upon her return to the United States: to establish an aviation school for the training of other African Americans from proceeds garnered by performing as a "barnstormer." Barnstorming was a term initially associated with theatre, and it referred to actors who traveled from city to city and town to town. Because in most cases there was nowhere for them to board, or lodge temporarily while on the performing circuit, they found the nearest barn to sleep in for the night, and by day they moved on to the next town to perform. By the early 1920s aeronautical barnstorming had become synonymous with adventuresome people, primarily unemployed former World War I fighter pilots, who flew surplus army aircraft for entertainment. These pilots would "buzz" a town in their aircraft--fly low to get the townspeople's attention and then fly off toward the nearest open field. There they would exhibit stunts of parachute jumping, wing-walking, low dives and dangerously daring flight maneuvers in the air. The performance usually culminated in the pilot's taking an eager passenger up for a brief ride in the plane for a fee of $1 to $5, depending on the reputation and the skill of the pilot. At day's end, the pilots would locate a barn in which to board themselves and the plane for the night.

Barnstorming was a prosperous enterprise during this time. If a barnstormer were an extraordinarily popular performer, his or her exhibition would be sponsored by a business or entrepreneur who recognized barnstorming as a profit making endeavor. The daredevils were making headlines daily, often for their adventuresome performances, and almost as often for the fatal crashes. Without air regulations, pilots flew however, whenever, and wherever they wanted to. While they entertained crowds of thousands they also endangered the lives of not only themselves, but their audience as well. The audience did not seem to mind, though, because Americans from all classes came out to the fairgrounds, circuses, cow pastures, parks, carnival grounds, and the ad hoc airstrips by the tens of thousands often on weekends for the spectacle and suspense of the experience that seemed to intensify their thirst for blood. Certain barnstormers were known to make as much as $1,000 a performance.[18]

Yet the profession was not without its stressful working conditions, and first on the list for many barnstormers seemed to be the antagonism of their audiences. Lincoln Beachey, "the World's Greatest Aviator," once gave up stuntflying and went into vaudeville, because he said, "I am convinced that the only thing that draws crowds to see me is the morbid desire to see something happen. They call me the 'Master Birdman,' but they pay to see me die."[19] Blanche Scott retired from avation at the age of twenty-seven, declaring that, "Too often, people paid money to see me risk my neck, more as a freak--a woman freak pilot--than as a skilled flier. No more!"[20] John Peer Nugent describes an unusual episode of morticians pursuing Hubert Julian an African American daredevil, before one aerial performance, harassing him for the rights to display his body should he crash.[21]

Coleman was extraordinary--she was an African American woman with an international pilot's license that allowed her to fly in any part of the world, and she was hailed by airmen and aircraft engineers in France, Germany, Holland and Switzerland "as the greatest aviatrix in the world, even surpassing the marvelous record made by the famous Ruth Law."[22] *The Chicago Defender* was now her sponsor, and she had established headquarters at their New York offices on Seventh Avenue as a base for booking her barnstorming exhibitions.

For her premiere performance, Coleman orchestrated a program that would appeal to prevailing public patriotism in general, and specifically to African American nationalism by honoring the 15th regiment.[23] The segregated 15th regiment, comprised primarily of musicians and theatre practitioners, was the first African American regiment sent to France during World War I. They were later designated the 369th Regiment 93rd Infantry Division, but retained the Fifteenth Regimental Band which was conducted by bandmaster Lieutenant James Reese Europe, and Drum Major Noble Sissle. This band was renowned for introducing brass-band jazz throughout Europe. Prior to his military stint, James Reese Europe was pianist, arranger and composer for Irene and Vernon Castle, the celebrated dancing team who shared their diluted version of African American dance with white American society at cabarets and supper clubs. International and national newspaper coverage of Coleman's aeronautical exploits in Europe, coupled with an extensive publicity campaign launched by the *Chicago Defender*, virtually ensured attendance by a substantially diverse audience for Coleman's first exhibition flight in the United States. In addition, Coleman's astute sense of what types of stunts and showmanship would please an audience seemed certain to ensure repeat performances.

On September 3, 1922, Coleman wearing O.D. (Officer of the Day) breeches, a Sam Brown belt, and a French officers jacket, was escorted to her airplane, by Captain E. C. McVey, after the band had concluded the "Star Spangled Banner." The location was the Curtiss Airfield in Garden City, Long Island; Curtiss Airplane Company provided Coleman's airplane for this event.[24] An integrated audience of several thousand watched in anticipation as Coleman, at 4:45 p.m, with McVey as passenger, took her Curtiss C-2 into a *chandelle* spiral upward into the air--"a maximum rate climbing turn during which the aeroplane traced the path of a rising half-loop whilst executing a banked turn through 180 degrees."[25] Several minutes later she landed, depositing her passenger on the airfield before continuing the second part of her performance. Coleman glided into what appeared to be the show's conclusion, but upon landing, another man dressed in a bright red outfit joined her in the cockpit.

The man was Hubert Fauntleroy Julian, an officer of Garvey's Universal Negro Improvement Association of New York. Julian was a flamboyant, wealthy, adventuresome young man born in Port of Spain, Trinidad a year after Coleman's birth. He had arrived in Harlem in July 1921 by way of Canada, with the intent of becoming a pilot. Julian had not yet earned the title of "Black Eagle." His aviation career was launched when he parachuted from the wing of Coleman's airplane at approximately 1,500-2,000 feet in the air during this event.[26] The audience was ecstatic. Coleman concluded her exhibition by taking individual passengers up in her plane for a $5.00 fee. "Only one passenger could be taken at a time, but five other planes were flying under the supervision of Miss Coleman, thereby giving those who wished an opportunity to be among the clouds for the first time."[27]

Coleman's pioneer performance generated interest in aviation among young African Americans who deluged her office seeking information on how to become pilots. She could only give them hope by sharing with them her dream of establishing a school for African Americans after she had saved enough money.[28] Bessie Coleman immediately engaged herself in preparation for her second show, that was to take place in her adopted hometown, Chicago.

The *Chicago Defender* billed Coleman as "The Only Race Aviatrix in the World," which doubtless summoned the more than 2,000 people who flocked to the Checkerboard Airdrome in Chicago, now Midway Airport, during her second exhibition on Sunday, October 15, 1922.[29] Once again, she honored an African American military regiment. This time it was the 8th regiment of Illinois; the second segregated National Guard unit to be shipped to France as the 370th Regiment, of the 93rd Infantry Division (Provisional) and the only one with African American officers.[30] This exhibition was divided into four parts. Coleman had delineated her planned program in newspaper advertisements, and according to press coverage of the event, she adhered to this program.[31] Many of the maneuvres she performed in this show bore the names of

World War I military aces—fighter pilots who had destroyed at least five enemy airplanes.

Their maneuvres emerged spontaneously, often while being pursued in the air by bullets from enemy aircraft--their stunts were born of their ingenuity in preserving their lives. For Coleman, however, it was a vehicle for some African Americans to enter mainstream America. The "French Nungesser start" with which Coleman began the first part of her second show was named after Captain Charles Nungesser, France's third-ranking World War I ace with forty-five victories.[32] For this stunt Coleman performed low level aerobatics by slightly leaving the ground and then dipping the plane close to the audience before ascending into the air. Dipping and flying low to the ground was a tactic frequently employed by barnstormers to elicit funds. She glided out of the Nungesser into a Spanish Bertha Costa climb, and immediately veered off into an American Curtiss-McMullen turn, straightening-up with an Eddie Rickenbacker, named after Captain Edward Vernon Rickenbacker, the United States' "Ace of Aces" credited with twenty-six victories.[33] From there she leveled into a Richthofen-German glide, named after Manfred von Richthofen, "The Red Baron," credited with eighty victories, and culminated in a Ralph C. Diggins landing, in honor of Chicagoan Ralph C. Diggins who had established a pilot training school at Ashburn Field in 1920.[34] The Eighth Regiment Band entertained the audience throughout with jazzy patriotic selections.[35]

After the intermission, Colonel Otis B. Duncan, commander of the 8th Illinois infantry escorted Coleman to her plane for the second part of the show, and the audience became ecstatic with surprise and excitement when he joined Coleman in the cockpit. Coleman climbed into a figure eight in honor of Duncan and his regiment, heightening audience suspense because the plane appeared to be out of control. But she foiled their expectations of sudden death before landing by banking, and making several low dips, as she had done at the beginning of the exhibition. The audience must have sighed a great sigh of relief as she leveled her plane into a smooth glide landing.

For the third part of her show, Coleman had her sister Georgia join her in the cockpit. Before taking off, she announced to the audience that Georgia would parachute from the plane at two thousand feet. An argument between the sisters ensued when Georgia refused to jump; Bessie had failed to discuss what parachuting entailed until the moment Georgia was to jump! Keeping with her patriotic theme, Coleman had had an elaborate costume made for Georgia in red, white, and blue in anticipation of Georgia's spectacular descent from the plane. Georgia, on the other hand, had merely thought her sister wanted her to look nice as a passenger and family member. Even though Georgia refused to jump, Coleman concluded the exhibition with several figure eights in the air before landing successfully.[36] Upon landing, Coleman presented the 8th regiment with an honor flag handmade by her.

Her next exhibition was sponsored by an African American realtor, Reynolds McKenzie, and took place in Gary Indiana. There, she met David Lewis Biencke, founder and President of the Air Line Pilots Association (International) who became her manager.[37] Coleman also took a purchasing trip in February 1923, to Coronado, California where she test-piloted and purchased three Curtiss airplanes from the Supply Division at the Air Intermediate Depot at Coronado.[38] Although the *Air Service News Letter* that reported this does not say why she purchased three airplanes, it can be assumed that these planes were in preparation for her establishment of a "flying air circus," since it was shortly after this trip that Coleman publicly announced her plan to barnstorm the South. Flying Circuses were comprised of either a group of stunt pilots who performed as barnstormers or pilots who executed a show directed by the celebrity pilot.[39] The latter arrangement is similar to the relationship between director and actor in theatre and film. It was also the prevalent practice among aerial barnstorming where the cost of one star was probably prohibitive, and, as in theatre and film, only one celebrity is actually needed to attract an audience. "The usual procedure was for a flying circus to book a concession at a fair or other outdoor event, where it would put on an 'air show' in return for the exclusive privilege of taking passengers."[40] Coleman had already begun to supervise the flight of other pilots during her exhibitions as indicated during an earlier show cited above.

Meanwhile, Biencke continued to schedule her in the Midwest area. She returned to perform in Columbus, Ohio, from where she received letters of welcome in anticipation of her arrival, from both the Governor of the state of Ohio and the Mayor of the City of Columbus. In a letter dated August 27, 1923, Governor Vic Donahey wrote:

Dear Miss Coleman:--

The committee in charge of the Labor Day Celebration in the City of Columbus inform [sic] me that you are to be present and assist in the proper observance of that day.

Therefore I extend to you a hearty welcome to the State of Ohio and to the City of Columbus, and trust your stay may be both pleasant and profitable.

Very truly yours,
VIC DONAHEY,
Governor.[41]

And the Mayor James J. Thomas wrote:

Dear Miss Coleman:--

Word comes to me that you are to pay us a visit on next Monday to aid in the observance of Labor Day.

Being familiar with your career and the skill, daring and courage you have exhibited on so many occasions and knowing how your efforts have been recognized by the heads of many European governments, I deem it an honor and a privilege to welcome you to the City of Columbus.

With the hope that your stay in our city will be pleasant and profitable, and again expressing my gratification that you are to visit us, I am,

Sincerely Yours,

JAS. J. THOMAS,

Mayor.[42]

After monumental success with her exhibitions throughout the Midwest, Coleman returned to Chicago for what the *Chicago Defender* reported would be her final performance in that part of the country. After that, she planned to barnstorm and lecture in the South to encourage African American participation in aviation.[43] Coleman's decision to concentrate her exhibits in the South resulted in a break in her relationship with Biencke, who believed that given the racist climate in the South, such an endeavor would be suicidal for Coleman's career, if indeed not for Coleman. Neither would compromise on this issue, so Biencke withdrew his services as Coleman's manager. It was a break, but with mutual respect of each for the other's decision and accomplishments.[44]

Coleman, already having experienced racism in both the North and South, did not heed his advice. Not only had she survived the Chicago race riots of 1919, she had recently returned from Columbus, Ohio where there had been a well-publicized Ku Klux Klan recruitment drive at the Ohio Fairgrounds, on the same day and in the same location that she was scheduled to perform.[45] She was an African American Southerner, who had made her home in the North, a place that still had about it a haze of golden opportunities as the promised land of the Great Migration. But Coleman had experienced the reality of living in Chicago where, in spite of the existence of a protective Civil Rights Law (1885), white proprietors arbitrarily denied service to African Americans in restaurants, hotels, theaters, stores, and other public establishments.[46] In her own neighborhood there had been "fifty-eight bombings of residences occupied by Negroes" during the period of July 1, 1917, to March 1, 1921.[47] The uncertainty of not knowing how she was going to be treated or received from one day to the next in the North, coupled with her objective to recruit African Americans into the field of aviation, compelled her to return South to barnstorm where the majority of African Americans still lived. Southern racial exclusionary practices were more consistent; African Americans knew the boundaries of Southern racism. These criteria may have abetted Coleman in her decision to travel on the T.O.B.A. circuit that catered to the entertainment needs of Southern Blacks. She booked lecture tours on the T.O.B.A. circuit, especially at movie theatres which were featuring screenings of newsreel footage of her stuntflying.

Shortly thereafter, she went to Houston, Texas set up headquarters and began to book her own exhibitions. One of her first performances there took place at the Aerial Transportation Field of that city. After Houston, she was scheduled to perform in her childhood town, at the Waxachatchie Airport. Coleman vociferously objected to audience segregation at this event and refused to perform unless African Americans were permitted to enter in the same gate as whites. The authorities acquiesced, and African Americans were admitted in the same gate, although they were shuttled into separate viewing sections once on the field.[48] Coleman continued on to Austin, Texas where, after her performance, a dinner was held in her honor, hostessed by another pioneer, Miriam A. ("Ma") Ferguson, then the first woman Governor in the United States.[49] Ferguson had won a landslide victory four years after the ratification of the Nineteenth Amendment, including as one of the key planks in her political platform an anti-Ku Klux Klan agenda, after her husband James E. Ferguson lost the Governor's seat under a political cloud.[50] In Wharton, Texas, Coleman hired Elizia Delworth, a white woman, to parachute from her plane during the exhibition--only to have a repeat performance of her sister Georgia's act: once in the air, the woman refused to jump. Coleman concluded this exhibition by jumping herself while Delworth flew the plane.[51]

Coleman continued across the South. In Memphis, Tennessee, she performed at the annual State Fair, where she was the featured attraction for an interracial audience. During this exhibit she slowly climbed the plane into the air and began to loop, and for a few seconds her plane appeared to be frozen in the air. Coleman circled back down toward the airfield and made a smooth landing. Although her flight was unusually short, the crowd did not seem to notice--they were elated. One young boy, however managed to sneak through Coleman's security barriers, and walked right up to her and asked "Lady, didn't your plane stop up there for a little while?" A surprised Coleman, admitted that the plane had faltered, and the youngster satisfied with his astute observation, smiled and walked off the field.[52] For a moment, her engine had indeed shut off or faltered in the air.

In addition to barnstorming in her airplanes at county fairs throughout the South, Coleman also barnstormed African American schools, churches, recreation facilities, and movie theatres to give lectures and show films of her aeronautical exploits to young people to whet their appetites for aviation. Donations were collected at these events as a contribution for the building of Coleman's aviation training school for African Americans.[53] During this time, Coleman also found the time to go back East, where one Sunday afternoon thousands of spectators saw her fly a memorial flight in honor of Harriet Quimby (1884-1912), over the Saint Charles River in Boston where Quimby fatally crashed.[54]

In 1924, Bessie Coleman returned to California where she was employed by the Firestone Tire Company in Santa Monica, to fly a plane advertising their product. That Firestone was willing to hire her was another important accomplishment further substantiating Coleman's success as aerialist. Sometime during the latter part of 1924, she had her first crash. In California, she fell 300 feet, giving her facial lacerations, three broken ribs, and a double fracture of the left leg which confined her to a hospital for several weeks.[55] Coleman returned to Chicago from California shortly after she was released from the hospital.

She spent the remainder of 1924 and almost half of 1925 recuperating at home, during which time she was romanced by the controversial Prince Kojo Touvalou-Houénou, of Dahomey, Africa.[56] Prince Kojo, a personal friend to both Robert Abbott and Marcus Garvey, was a Black nationalist, a lawyer, and presently the Potentate (leader; elected in 1924) of Garvey's U.N.I.A. and

> a member of the family of Behanzin, deposed King of Dahomey whom the French had exiled to Algeria. He was born in Africa, educated in Europe, and was fluent in French, German and English.... His friends included titled personages, officers of the army and navy, actors and actresses, painters and singers.[57]

Coleman's nieces who lived with her during her convalescence remembered that he was always around and they called him Mr. Prince.[58]

It is not known what happened to their relationship, but it is safe to speculate that Coleman's freedom was indispensable to her. Her niece, Marion Coleman, who was a youngster at the time, remembers that while the family was not in the "habit of discussing each other's love lives," they did occasionally mention a Mr. Grant Mitchell and a Mr. Glenn, supposedly two husbands that Bessie had married, only to leave them shortly thereafter in pursuit of her career. No official records that would ascertain Coleman's marital status have been unearthed. Bessie Coleman was not alone in her refusal to be tied down. While the "New Negro" of the era presented in most historical texts is decidedly male, African American women were reshaping their lives with a feminist (or, to use Alice Walker's term, "womanist") agenda. For example, two of Bessie Coleman's contemporaries, Alberta Hunter and Josephine Baker, both married in their teens and immediately left their spouses. Baker sailed on an oceanliner for Paris within a month after her marriage; and Hunter was to state many times during her career that she just wasn't cut out to be "nobody's housewife."

Marion Coleman informed this writer that as much as Bessie loved her mother, "when she had to go, she had to go. She didn't sit around waiting for nobody to be married and all that stuff."[59] Marion Coleman recalls that Bessie had suitors who spoke in different languages, especially around the children. Bessie could speak Spanish, French, and German. Evidently her quadri-lingual capabilities, her light skinned coloring, and her exotic wardrobe, purchased in Europe, prompted more than one reporter from the *Chicago Tribune* to encourage Coleman to pass--to pretend that she was an exotic foreigner rather than an African American. But she would instead summon her mother, and admonish them to note her dark complexion, and her African American features, making it emphatically clear that although she could have passed, she had no desire to. Coleman was too much of an African American nationalist to pursue that route. At any rate, during the middle of 1925, Coleman resumed daily practice flights and soon after cast off her Chicago beau Prince Kojo, as she probably had the husbands earlier, and renewed her aviation career.

Coleman must have been sufficiently well enough to travel and lecture, if not to perform, because she was back on the lecture trail by May 5, 1925. The *Houston Post Dispatch* reports on that date that Coleman was to appear that evening at the temple of the Independent Order of Odd Fellows (I. O. O. F.) to lecture and screen films of her American and European aerial exploits. Coleman's obsession to undermine the "Uncle Tom" image is once again manifest in her statement during this interview that she intended "to make Uncle Tom's Cabin into a hangar."[60] The hangar, of course, is where she would park her plane, and, thus, naming her hangar Uncle Tom would be a symbolic act. The cabin, formerly an index of the captivity of African American slaves, would become the lodging for their ticket, literally, to the sky as the limit. "[T]oward this end," the newspaper report continued, "she plans to establish a flying school and teach the negro [sic] to fly so that they can be better citizens and will be able to serve their country better."[61]

After leaving Houston, she returned to Chicago to spend the Christmas holidays with family. Her family tried to convince her to give up aviation during this visit. This was not the first time they tried to get her to stop, but it was a more concerted effort because they felt that the stall in mid-air in Tennessee, and the fall in California, were omens that it was time for her to stop. Coleman vehemently refused, suggesting that to give her life for the advancement of her race would be an honor, and stated that "if they can but create the minimum of my plans and desires there shall be no regrets."[62] She spent Christmas day with her sister Elois who altered an evening dress for her. When she left later that day, it was the last time Elois was to see her alive.

Coleman went to live with friends in Orlando, Florida during the winter of 1926, where she continued speaking engagements for small donations in African American churches, theatres and schools. Although Coleman needed larger sums of money to establish her aviation school, her loyalty to her race would not permit her to compromise her integrity. She turned down the Orlando Chamber of Commerce in March of that year when she learned that African Americans would be excluded from attending her performance. Coleman angrily sent her plane back to Texas. Even when the white businessmen relented, Coleman did not agree to perform until "the Jim Crow order had been revoked and aviators had been sent up to drop placards letting the members of our Race know they could come into the field."[63] Shortly after this engagement, Coleman was hired by the Negro Welfare League in Jacksonville, Florida to perform at their annual 1st of May Field Day. Coleman was so honored that an esteemed African American organization had invited her to perform that she accepted the invitation without hesitation. Whereas many African Americans were proud of her and would come to her exhibitions in large numbers, none of their organizations had yet financially supported her endeavor to build a school. With this invitation she believed she would obtain the serious backing that had thus far eluded her, thereby placing her objective within reach. Coleman wrote a letter to her sister Elois at this time stating that she was "right on the threshold of opening a school."[64]

Coleman had trouble however, locating an airplane in Florida because dealers would not sell, rent, or loan an African American an airplane in this region.[65] When she had exhausted her options, she contacted her white mechanic, William D. Wills in Dallas, Texas and summoned him to fly a plane to her for the impending performance. "Edwin W. Beeman, sole heir of the millionaire gum manufacturer," put up the $500.00 to transport Colemans' plane from Texas to Jacksonville.[66] Wills, her twenty-four year old mechanic arrived in Jacksonville from Dallas on Wednesday April 28, in an airplane he had obtained from the Curtiss Airplane and Motor Company.[67]

John T. Betsch, Coleman's Florida publicity manager, a Howard graduate interested in aeronautics, and member of the Jacksonville Negro Welfare League, accompanied Coleman and Wills at 7:15 A.M. to the Paxon Airfield on Friday, April 30 for a dress rehearsal of the impending performance.[68] Before entering the cockpit, Coleman knelt in prayer beside the aircraft. When she arose she promised to take

Betsch up after she test piloted the plane. Wills was piloting the plane as a few spectators watched the plane soaring in graceful patterns against the early morning sun. Suddenly the graceful circles turned into wildly, uncontrolled circles and the plane began to descend rapidly from the air into a sharp nosedive toward the ground. Bessie Coleman was catapulted out of the machine at about 2,000 feet when the plane somersaulted in several revolutions; she was not wearing a seatbelt or a parachute. When her body was found in a farmyard owned by Mrs. W. L. Meadows almost a mile from where the plane crashed, every bone in her body had been crushed by the impact.[69]

As the plane continued to descend toward earth, Wills remained with it, secured by a seatbelt. He righted the plane, and just as it appeared that he might land safely the plane collided with the top of a pine tree, bouncing off and hitting the ground with a thud. John T. Betsch rushed to the site where in his excitement he struck a match to light a cigarette, igniting the gasoline fumes surrounding the plane. The aircraft burst into flame and Wills was cremated inside. Betsch was arrested by police, but after several hours of interrogation, he was released because no malice was found to be evident in his actions; they were attributed to nervous confusion generated by the crash. It was later discovered that Wills, an employee of the Southern Aircraft company at Dallas, and supposed veteran of fifty-seven flights, had made two forced landings enroute from Dallas to Jacksonville because of engine trouble.

Some African Americans believed that white people had sabotaged Coleman's airplane. They blamed Wills for Coleman's death, based on a piece of circumstantial evidence: Robert Abbott was overheard the day before the crash in a restaurant warning Coleman not to go up in an airplane with Wills because "he didn't like the looks of the Texan."[70] Those who subscribed to the theory that Wills was the culprit also pointed out that after Coleman was thrown clear of the plane during its nosedive, he had been able to regain control of the plane. Wills would have survived the mishap had he not collided with a tree, and had Betsch not chosen the wrong moment to light a cigarette.

However, accusations pointing at malice on the part of the dead Wills were somewhat dispelled by the discovery of a wrench in the wreckage of Coleman's airplane. The wrench was found jammed in the control gears, where it was doubtless responsible for the abrupt nose dive in the air.[71] Wills, so the revised scenario went, could not have been directly responsible for the crash. Since the location of the wrench was not accessible from the cockpit, Wills would have had to have positioned it before takeoff. But if the wrench had been in place while the plane was on the ground, it would have been impossible to pilot the plane into the air. More likely, investigators finally concluded, was that Wills as mechanic had absentmindedly left a wrench somewhere near the control gears inside the plane while it was on the ground. After takeoff, while the plane was rolling and diving, the wrench slid into the gears and jammed them. Still, it was impossible to verify or discredit this story, particularly about whether Wills was merely careless, or whether he had engineered the accident.

The magnitude of Coleman's impact and importance to Black America was manifested in three funerals held for her, which were attended and presided over by some of the most distinguished members of the Black community. For Black people funerals were the ultimate way of displaying admiration. (Those of Florence Mills [1927], A'Leilia Walker [1931], Bill Bojangles Robinson and others are legendary).[72] Coleman's were attended by young and old, black and white, rich and poor. She had endeared herself to these diverse communities during her brief stay in Orlando and Jacksonville, Florida, by speaking at theatres, churches, elementary and secondary schools.[73] Some had been introduced to her through newspaper accounts of the numerous activities held in her honor. In order to accommodate the large number of this diverse group in paying their last respects to Coleman, her remains lay in state at the Lawton L. Pratt Undertaker parlors in Jacksonville where people filed through Saturday, May 1 until after midnight, after which her remains were forwarded by train on Sunday, May 2 to Orlando where she had previously spent some time resting for her health.[74] In Orlando the funeral was held at Mt. Zion Baptist Church at eleven o'clock Monday morning May 3, where Reverend H. K. Hill gave the sermon. A soloist sang "I've Done My Work," and the choir sang "Lead, Kindly Light." When the service had ended, pallbearers ushered the body into the waiting hearse on its way to the train depot where the Illinois Central Railroad would carry "Brave Bessie" on her final journey to Chicago. Coleman's remains, accompanied by Mrs. H. K. Hill, wife of Rev. H. K. Hill, pastor of the Mt. Zion Baptist church at Orlando, arrived in Chicago Wednesday, May 5, and were taken to the Kersey, McGowan & Morsell Funeral parlor where she lay in state while an estimated 10,000 people passed by to pay their respects until the final funeral on Friday, May 7.[75]

The funeral services began at 10 A.M. Friday morning at the Pilgrim Baptist Church. Six pallbearers, veterans of the Illinois 8th regiment, solemnly marched up the aisle of the large church bearing Coleman's flag-draped casket, followed by twenty-four honorary pallbearers, comprised of Chicago's leading citizens:

Attorney Wendell E. Green, Dr. Midian O. Bousfield, Major Adam Patterson, Attorney Earl B. Dickerson, Major N. Clark Smith, Oscar DePriest, Hon. Warren B. Douglas, Cry B. Lewis, Dr. Albert J. Northcross, Attorney Van O. DeSuse, Attorney Chester C. Horn, Dr. Jesse Trice, Dr. McCaskill, David W. Kellum, Perry C. Thompson, A. J. Gary, Louis

Branch, Harvey A. Watkins, Dr. Robbie Giles, Lucius C. Harper, Leslie M. Rogers and Dr. A. Wilberforce Williams.[76]

Reverend Junius Caesar Austin, Sr. (1887-1968) pastor of the church, and Reverend C. M. Tanner, pastor of Greater Bethel church, officiated at the Chicago funeral. They were assisted by the Reverends Schell, assistant pastor. The choir sang "Jesus, Savior, Pilot Me," and after Colonel Otis B. Duncan, commander of the 8th regiment reminisced on the flight he took with Coleman during her debut performance in Chicago in 1922, Ida B. Wells-Barnett, mistress of ceremonies, recalled the first time she had personally met with Bessie Coleman. Coleman had visited Wells-Barnett's home in Chicago shortly after her return from her first sojourn to Europe "to express gratitude for the first and only letter of congratulation she had received from Chicago, since returning to her native land."[77] Throughout the ceremonies Coleman was repeatedly described as an unselfish, indomitable, courageous woman with extraordinary intelligence and integrity. Both Reverends Austin and Tanner stressed Coleman's loyalty to the African American race, stating that although Coleman had been "offered substantial sums to give exhibitions exclusively for the other race, she steadily refused to accept them unless her people were allowed admission."[78] And both ministers emphasized the tragedy of ungratefulness from the same group of people, with Austin concluding that "this girl was 100 years ahead of the Race she loved so well, and by whom she was least appreciated."[79] His critical remarks were prompted by his recognition that while African Americans strongly admired "Brave Bessie" and supported her as audience members, few supported her financially, which is where backing really mattered. The Reverends Austin and Tanner, and Ross D. Brown, among others, believed that this lack of financial support forced her to rely on whatever airplanes, management, and financial support she could muster in order to pursue her endeavor. And in the final analysis this lack of support, in effect, may have hastened her premature death. Bessie Coleman was buried in Lincoln Cemetery founded by and for African Americans in 1911 in response to discrimination and exclusion by white cemetary owners.[80] Coleman's grave lay unmarked until Memorial Day, 1927 when the Cooperative Business Men's League, of Cook County, Illinois and Florida Friends presented a headstone in her honor that reads:

IN MEMORY OF
BESSIE COLEMAN
ONE OF THE FIRST AMERICAN
WOMEN TO ENTER THE FIELD OF

AVIATION. REMEMBERED FOR
COURAGE AND ACCOMPLISHMENTS.
SHE FELL 5,300 [sic] FEET WHILE FLY-
ING AT JACKSONVILLE, FLORIDA,
APRIL 30, 1926.
PRESENTED BY
CO-OPERATIVE BUSINESS LEAGUE
COOK COUNTY ILL AND FLORIDA FRIENDS[81]

Notes

1. "Aviatrix Must Sign Away Life To Learn Trade," *Chicago Defender* 8 October 1921: 2.

2. Marianna Davis, ed., *Contributions of Black Women to America*, Vol. I (South Carolina: Kenday Press, Inc., 1982) 498.

3. *Chicago Defender* 8 October 1921: 2.

4. *Chicago Defender* 8 October 1921: 2.

5. *Chicago Defender* 8 October 1921: 2.

6. David Young and Neal Callahan, *Fill The Heavens with Commerce: Chicago Aviation 1855-1926* (Chicago: Chicago Review Press, 1981) 67.

7. *Chicago Defender* 8 October 1921: 2.

8". "'Shuffle Along' Company Gives Fair Flyer Cup," *Chicago Defender* 8 October 1921: 2.

9. "Chicago Colored Girl Learns to Fly Abroad," *Chicago Tribune*, 26 September 1921: N. pag.; "Chicago Girl Is a Full-Fledged Aviatrix Now," *Chicago Defender* 1 October 1921: 1; "Aviatrix Must Sign Away Life To Learn Trade," *Chicago Defender* 8 October 1921: 2; "Negro Aviatrix to Tour the Country," Air Service News Letter, Vol. 5, 1 November 1921: 11; *The Half-Century Magazine: A Colored Magazine for the Home and Homemaker* November, 1921: 6; "Chicago Colored Girl Learns to Fly Abroad," Aerial Age Weekly, 17 October 1921: 125.

10. "Chicago Colored Girl Learns to Fly Abroad," *Chicago Tribune*, 26 September 1921: N. pag.; "Chicago Girl Is a Full-Fledged Aviatrix Now," *Chicago Defender* 1 October 1921: 1; "Aviatrix Must Sign Away Life To Learn Trade," *Chicago Defender* 8 October 1921: 2; "Negro Aviatrix to Tour the Country," Air Service News Letter, Vol. 5, 1 November 1921: 11; *The Half-Century Magazine: A Colored Magazine for the Home and Homemaker* November, 1921: 6; "Chicago Colored Girl Learns to Fly Abroad," Aerial Age Weekly, 17 October 1921: 125.

11. John Heritage, *The Wonderful World of Aircraft* (London: Octopus Books Limited, 1980) 20.

12. Janet Harmon Bragg (née Waterford) telephone interview with Elizabeth Hadley Freydberg 9 April 1988; Mary Oglesby personal interview with Elizabeth Hadley Freydberg 13 August 1989.

13. See "The Rollicking Barnstormers," in *The Challenging Skies: The Colorful Story of Aviation's Most Exciting Years 1919-1939*, by C. R. Roseberry, 44. This work documents that, Charles Lindbergh, known as "The Flying Fool" during his early barnstorming days also performed this stunt as indicated by a poster that read "See 'Bud'

Lindbergh Stop His Motor 3000 Feet in the Air, Landing with Engine Dead!" See also Judy Lomax's Women of the Air 164, indicates that this was a popular stunt among some women in "flying circuses."

14. "Negro Aviatrix Arrives: Bessie Coleman Flew Planes of Many Types in Europe," *The New York Times*14 August 1922: 4; "Negress in Flying Show: Bessie Coleman to Give Exhibition for Fifteenth Regiment," *The New York Times* 27 August 1922: 2.

15. John Heritage, *The Wonderful World of Aircraft* (London: Octopus Books Limited, 1980) 20.

16. "Negro Aviatrix Arrives: Bessie Coleman Flew Planes of Many Types in Europe," *The New York Times*, August 14 1922; "Bessie to Fly Over Gotham: Queen Bess to Ride Air Next Sunday," *Chicago Defender* 26 August 1922: 1.

17. *The New York Times* 14 August 1922: 4.

18. James H. Farmer, *Broken Wings: Hollywood's Air Crashes*. (Montana: Pictorial Histories Publishing Company, 1984) 7.

19. Sherwood Harris, *The First To Fly: Aviation's Pioneer Days*. (New York: Simon and Schuster, 1970) 287.

20. *Judy Lomax, Women of the Air*, (New York: Dodd, Mead & Company, 1987) 27.

21. John Peer Nugent, *The Black Eagle* (New York: Stein and Day Publishers, 1971) 33. An excellet account of the life of this daredevil pilot, inventor, parachutist and entrepenuer.

22. "Bessie to Fly Over Gotham: Queen Bess to Ride Air Next Sunday" *Chicago Defender* 26 August 1922: 1; Kathleen Brooks-Pazmany, United States Women in Aviation 1919-1929, Smithsonian Studies in Air and Space No. 5 (Washington, D. C.: Smithsonian Institution Press, 1983) 9. Law was a white woman whose expert stunt flying earned her the reputation as a daredevil of the sky; she won many honors for breaking and establishing flight records, and she is credited with launching night time air mail between Chicago and New York.

23. For a more comprehensive discussion of this regiment and its contributions to the United States see Emmett J. Scott, The American Negro in the World War (Washington, D.C., 1919); "Two Black Fighting Outfits," The Unknown Soldiers: Black American Troops in World War I, 70-88; and John Hope Franklin, "In Pursuit of Democracy," *From Slavery to Freedom: A History of Negro Americans*, 452-476.

24. "Bessie Gets Away; Does Her Stuff," *Chicago Defender* 9 September 1922: 3.

25. The description of a chandelle is taken from Flight Fantastic: *The Illustrated History of Aerobatics* by Annette Carson, (England: Haynes Publishing Group, 1986) 37.

26. "Negress Pilots Airplane," *The New York Times* 4 September 1922: 9; "Bessie Coleman Shows 'Em How," *Afro-American* 8 September 1922: 1; *Chicago Defender* 9 September 1922: 3.

27. Blaine Poindexter, "Bessie Coleman Makes Initial Aerial Flight: Chicagoans See Girl Who Flew Over Berlin in Series of Stunts," *Chicago Defender* 21 October 1922: 3.

28. *Chicago Defender* 9 September 1922: 3.

29. Poindexter, *Chicago Defender* 21 October 1922: 3.

30. Arthur E. Barbeau and Florette Henri, *The Unknown Soldiers: Black American Troops in World War I* (Philadelphia: Temple University Press, 1974) 75.

31. Advertisement, *Chicago Defender* 14 October 1922: 3.

32. Poindexter, *Chicago Defender* 21 October 1922: 3.

33. Poindexter, *Chicago Defender* 21 October 1922: 3.

34. *Chicago Defender* 9 September 1922: 3; Poindexter, *Chicago Defender* 21 October 1922: 3.

35. *Chicago Defender* 9 September 1922: 3.

36. *Bessie Coleman Memoirs*, N. pag.

37. *Bessie Coleman Memoirs*, N. pag.

38. "Colored Aviatrix Bobs Up Again," *Air Service News Letter*, Vol. 7, February 20, 1923: 4.

39. C. R. Roseberry, *The Challenging Skies: The Colorfoul Story of Aviations's Most Exciting Years 1919* (New York: Doubleday & Company, Inc., 1966) 41.

40. Roseberry, 41-43.

41 Courtesy of the Black Film Center Archive. Professor Phyllis R. Klotman, Director. Indiana University, Bloomington.

42. Courtesy of the Black Film Center Archive.

43. "Plans Flight," *Chicago Defender* 22 September 1923: 2.

44. Biencke's son provided me with a copy of the *Bessie Coleman Memoirs* in 1985, stating that he felt relieved to do so, because before his father died he had charged him with the responsibility of passing it on to someone who would publish Coleman's story.

45. "Aviatrix to Fly at Driving Park," and "Gigantic Klonvocation Knights and Ladies of the Ku Klux Klan," *The Columbus Dispatch* 2 September 1923: 2 and 38. The same newspaper reported "Klan Initiates 2300 at Monday Meeting," 4 September 1923: 18..

46. Allan H Spear, *Black Chicago: The Making of a Negro Ghetto 1890-1920* (Chicago: The University of Chicago Press, 1967) 206.

47. Arna Bontemps and Jack Conroy, *Anyplace But Here.* Originally published as *They Seek a City* (1945; New York: Hill and Wang, 1966) 176.

Marjorie Kriz, "Bessie Coleman, Aviation Pioneer," *U. S. Department of Transportation News* (U. S. Department of

Transportation Federal Aviation Administration Office of Public Affairs, Great Lakes Region, n.d.) 3.

49. St. Laurent, Philip, "Bessie Coleman, Aviator," *Washington Sunday Star Tuesday Magazine* January 1973: N. Pag.; "Brave Bessie: First Black Pilot in U. S. Was A Lady," *FAA General Aviation News*, January-February 1983: 17.

50. For a historical account of the political life of Miriam A. ("Ma") Ferguson see Jack Lynn Calbert's "James Edward and Miriam Amanda Ferguson: The 'Ma' and 'Pa' of Texas Politics," diss., Indiana U/Bloomington, 1968.

51. Bessie Coleman Memoirs, N. pag.; Philip St. Laurent, "Bessie Coleman: Aviator," *Washington Sunday Star, Tuesday Magazine* January 1973: N. pag.

52. *Memoirs*, N. pag.

53. "Texas Negro Girl Becomes Able Aviatrix," *Houston Post Dispatch* 7 May 1925: 4.

54. *Memoirs*, N. pag.; Philip St. Laurent, January 1973: N. pag.

55. *Houston Post Dispatch* 7 May 1925: 4; "Body of Bird Girl On Way to Chicago: Funeral to Be Held Friday Morning" 31 May 1926, unidentified newsclipping, in "Black Aviators" File, Schomburg Center Clipping File, New York Public Library.

56. Patrick Manning and James S. Speigler, "Kojo Tovalou-Houenou: Franco-Dahomean Patriot." Unpublished paper, presented at the African Studies Association annual meeting, Chicago, November 1988. This is the most comprehensive study of this controversial prince.

57. Roi Ottley, "A Man Called Kojo," *The Lonely Warrior* (Chicago: Henry Regnery Company, 1955) 289; Claude McKay, *Harlem: Negro Metropolis* (New York: Harcourt Brace Jovanovich, Inc., 1968) 168-69; Theodore G. Vincent, *Black Power and the Garvey Movement* (San Francisco, 1971) 158.

58. Vera Buntin, telephone interview with Elizabeth Hadley Freydberg, 12 January 1985.

59. Marion Coleman, personal interview 12 January 1985.

60. *Houston Post Dispatch* 7 May 1925: 4.

61. *Houston Post Dispatch* 7 May 1925: 4.

62. *Coleman Memoirs*, N. pag.

63. "Florida Mayor Drinks Toast to 'Brave Bess,'" *Chicago Defender* 15 May 1926: 2. Mrs. Viola T. Hill, president of the Florida Women's Baptist Convention, Bessie Coleman's "god-mother" and hostess during her stay in Orlando recounts this incident in this article.

64. *Coleman Memoirs*, N. pag.

65. "'Bird' Woman Falls 2,000 Feet To Death," *The Baltimore Afro-American* 8 May 1926: 1.

66. E. B. Jourdain, Jr., "Two Lives Snuffed Out When Plane Crashes Down," *Chicago Defender* 8 May 1926: 3.

67. "'Bird' Woman Falls 2,000 Feet To Death," *The Baltimore Afro-American*, 8 May 1926: 1.

68 Herbert Aptheker, and Robert Hall, historians indicated to me in 1992 that believed Betsch to be the father of Dr. Johnnetta Betsch Cole, President of Spelman College. Aptheker questioned Cole in my behalf and her letter of 15 March 1992 forwarded to me states that she has no "specific information about Bessie Coleman or my [her] father's relationship with her."

69. "Bessie Coleman and White Pilot in 2000 Ft. Crash," *The New York Amsterdam News* 5 May 1926: 1.

70. "Plane Falls 2000 Feet: 'Bird' Woman Falls 2,000 Feet To Death," *The Afro-American*, [City Edition] 8 May 1926: 1; Bessie Coleman Memoirs, N. pag; Philip St. Laurent, "Bessie Coleman, Aviator," *Washington Sunday Star Tuesday Magazine* January 1973: N. Pag.

71. "Body of Bird Girl On Way to Chicago: Funeral to be Held Friday Morning," Jacksonville 31 May 1926, unidentified newsclipping, in "Black Aviators" File, Schomburg Center Clipping File, New York Public Library; E. B. Jourdain, Jr. "Bessie Coleman, Aviatrix, Killed: 'Two Lives Snuffed Out When Plane Crashes Down,'" *Chicago Defender* 8 May 1926: 1-3; "Bessie Coleman and White Pilot in 2000 Ft. Crash: White Pilot's body Cremated in Wreckage When Eye-Witness Struck Match--Miss Coleman Toppled From Plane as It Somersaulted in Mid-Air," *The New York Amsterdam News* 5 May 1926: 1. "Plane Falls 2000 Feet: 'Bird' Woman Falls 2,000 Feet To Death," *The Baltimore Afro-American*, [City Edition] 8 May 1926: 1.

72. See Langston Hughes, "When Harlem Was in Vogue" *Town and Country* July 1940: 66, 64; James Weldon Johnson, *Black Manhattan* (1930; 1958; New York: Arno Press and *The New York Times*, 1968) 200-201.

73. "To Hold Funeral For Negro Aviatrix," *Orlando Morning Sentinel* 3 May 1926: 5; E. B. Jourdain, Jr., *Chicago Defender* 8 May 1926: 1.

74. E. B. Jourdain, Jr., *Chicago Defender* 8 May 1926: 1. This was not an unusual hour for working class African Americans. Langston Hughes' explanation for late night funerals in Harlem can be applied here and to many African American communities. He remarks that, "Since almost all Harlemites work in the daytime, many of the Harlem funerals take place at night so that the friends and lodge brothers of the deceased may attend. Sometimes at eleven at night you hear a funeral march filling the air on Seventh Avenue;" "When Harlem Was In Vogue," *Town & Country* July 1940: 66.

75. "Guardsmen to Bury Chicago Aviatrix," *Chicago Tribune* 5 May 1926; E. B. Jourdain, Jr., Chicago Defender 8 May 1926: 1.

76. Evangeline Roberts, "Chicago Pays Parting Tribute to 'Brave Bessie' Coleman," *Chicago Defender* 15 May 1926: 2.

77. Roberts, *Chicago Defender* 15 May 1926: 2.

78. Roberts, *Chicago Defender* 15 May 1926: 2.

79. Roberts, *Chicago Defender* 15 May 1926: 2.

80. Lincoln (1911) and Mount Glenwood (1908) Cemeteries were founded by African Americans in response to discrimination and exclusion by white cemetary owners; see Alan H. Spear, *Black Chicago: The Making of Negro Ghetto 1890-1920* (Chicago: The University of Chicago Press, 1967) 118.

81. Elizabeth Hadley Freydberg photographed this headstone, one of two that now grace Coleman's gravesite, on 19 March 1988.

V

"There Shall Be No Regrets"

She asked Negro business men to pool their funds and help to
motorize the sky. She received no reply, and was forced to
consider others who took an interest in her cause.

Ross D. Brown

Coleman was always short on funds; yet she was aware of current
cultural, social and political events and she exploited them in an effort
to slip African Americans into mainstream America. She equated herself
with Joan of Arc, incorporated herself into newsreels when they became
popular with audiences, planned her costumes and staged her
performances with specific audiences in mind. She was laying the
groundwork to have her life depicted in film, immortalized as popular
entertainment, at the time of her death. Coleman began to invoke the
name of Joan of Arc during interviews upon her return from her first
trip abroad. Her earliest references to the legendary French woman
warrior informed the public that she studied in "the city where Joan of
Arc was held prisoner by the English."[1] She began to don French
military uniforms for her performances, further reinforcing her spiritual
kinship with this fifteenth century Frenchwoman. Her use of Joan of
Arc as a persistent analogy and metaphor, combined with her uniforms,
conjured an equation between her own African American nationalism,
and the ardent nationalism of the Maid of Orleans. For it was Joan of
Arc who had been instrumental, in spirit if not in fact, in forging a
post-medieval country from a heterogeneous sequence of fiefdoms which
were more often than not engaged in internecine strife and petty
squabbles.

There were indeed several parallels in the lives of Joan of Arc and
Bessie Coleman. Both were near the same age when they endeavored to
change the course of history--Joan of Arc seventeen, Bessie Coleman
eighteen. Joan of Arc sought to free her people, the French, from
British tyranny and oppression; Coleman the African American sought

to free her people, from Anglo American racial tyranny and oppression. Against all odds each chose an avenue to make social changes, yet uncharted by women--Joan in the military, Coleman in the field of aviation. Joan of Arc was charged with heresy for hearing voices outside of the Roman Catholic cathedrals, and with lunacy for her decision to dress in male battle gear rather than the cumbersome long skirts deemed appropriate feminine attire. Coleman's inspirations which led her into the sky certainly appeared lunatic or moonstruck to some, although the fashion industry had evolved to a point where it could afford to wink at her eccentric habiliments. It is significant that Coleman began this correlation soon after Joan of Arc had been canonized a saint by the Roman Catholic Church on May 16, 1920 because it is once again an indication of Coleman's awareness of current cultural and political events governing her life and those of the larger society in which she lived.

Nevertheless that some people in the African American community did recognize the parallels in the lives of the two young patriotic nationalists is evident in a letter submitted to a Harlem apartment-naming contest a year after Coleman's death. The following winning letter was published in a newspaper article entitled "Harlem's Newest Apartments Named After Black 'Joan of Arc:'"

Dear Editor:
I am a weekly reader of your paper, and I am delighted to make the effort in suggesting a name for the new exclusive and luxurious apartment house. I have selected Bessie Coleman, our first and only aviatrix.
Recently New York City proclaimed its hero, Col. Charles Lindbergh. Therefore, it is befitting to our illustrious heroine, who fought for the same cause. But ended her career with an upward flight to the great beyond, only one year ago. It would be in memory of our deceased female eagle of the air.

Mrs.Nellie Harrison[2]

The Harlem apartment building was designated Coleman Manor.

Coleman arranged to have herself filmed, during her second trip to France in 1922, on newsreels--a film subgenre that materialized in 1896, the year of her birth. Coleman was employed by *Pathé News of America* to pilot photographers while they took aerial photos.[3] *Pathé* cameramen also filmed some "2000 Feet of Film Showing her Flights in Europe and America."[4] It was the only company who filmed her throughout her life, as far as can be determined and the film footage is now extinct.[5] These were the films that were shown in the African American movie theatres on the T.O.B.A. circuit. *Pathé* was the leading innovator in news films at this time, and had also established an American film studio in New Jersey (1910) to produce both newsreels and feature films.

News films by then were used very much as they are today--as brief visual documentation of events of the day. Just as melodrama attracted and exploited the action-packed script, so too news film captured the action of trains, boats, automobiles and airplanes. Newsreels remain today our foremost permanent record of these turn-of-the-century inventions.[6] Since mass communication was also at an embryonic stage and had not yet developed into the sophisticated channels as it has today, the news film was the vehicle that brought new inventions such as the airplane to the masses. All newspapers did not cover aviation events, and even when they did, the news film provided the public with another mode of access to these events. Further, even when they were reported, readers had to rely on accounts of events as seen through the eyes of randomly selected journalists. During the infant years of aviation, many reporters had no idea of what they were looking at. For example they could not adequately describe a barnstorming event unless the principals provided them, as Coleman did on occasion, with a complete program itemizing the names of the maneuvers she was about to perform.

Newsreels, then, provided actual documentation of the aviation event and authenticated Coleman as an international aviatrix. Such authenticity served her well upon her second return to the United States, as is documented in Chapter IV. In the United States newsreels had become an integral segment of the vaudeville bill in many theatres during the first part of the twentieth century. By the middle of the 1920s, Coleman's ten minute newsreels were shown during intermission and as finales in many of the vaudeville theatres on the African American circuit.[7]

Coleman intended to have her life reflected in the longer length entertainment films before she died. She had implemented plans to immortalize herself in celluloid during 1926, the year of her death. In a query letter dated February 3 that year, she stated to independent film producer and director Richard Norman that, "I have my life work that I want put into pictures....I am, and know it, the most known colored person (woman alive) other than the Jazz singers."[8] By the time Coleman had written this letter, she was clearly aware of the impact of film on American society. She also knew that it was a lucrative endeavor which would bring her financially closer to establishing an aviation school.

By Coleman's day, feature film had been an established form of entertainment, with its own structure and stylistic conventions, and with a box-office gross that was beginning to alarm the legitimate and vaudeville theatres. In 1900, French film producer and former theatre

magician Georges Melies, introduced a three-act film story to the screen
in France. It was based on the structure of the stage play, and became
the prototype for all films thereafter, including Melies' better-known *A
Trip to the Moon* (1902), the first narrative film.[9] Thomas Edison had
already invented the Kinetoscope (1891) in the United States. The bill
of fare for the Kinetoscope used some positive images of African
Americans, such as *Colored Troops Disembarking* (1898), and *The
Ninth Negro Cavalry Watering Horses* (1899). However, it had also
embraced negative stereotypes in *Watermelon Contest* (1899) and
Sambo and Aunt Jemima: Comedians (ca. 1897-1900),[10] which were to
prevail in American cinematic enterprises. In fact by 1926, the character
and subject of "Uncle Tom," stripped of any anti-slavery sentiment, had
been produced in film no less than seven times, with Edison producing
at least two--one in 1902, and one in 1909.[11] By 1907 the gross
income of approximately 5,000 permanent movie theatres throughout
the country "exceeded that of the legitimate theaters and vaudeville
combined."[12]

Other notable aviators had begun to take advantage of the medium
as early as 1908. The first aerial motion pictures were taken in France
from the wing of a Wright flyer in 1908, and featured the countryside
near LeMans.[13] Two years later former President Theodore Roosevelt
was filmed waving to people from the air in his first airplane ride.[14]
Movie moguls quickly seized upon the opportunity to make a profit
from aerial entertainment by filming the activities of some of the
pioneering stuntflyers and integrating the footage into their films. For
these enterprising entrepreneurs, aviation was "a natural source for the
kind of cinematic thrills that would fill box office coffers."[15] The
aviators were now compensated for risking their lives with reliable
income and mass public exposure, while the movie moguls profited
from their life-threatening risks whether the stuntflyer was killed or not
during a production. After all, a live show ending in the devoutly-
wished disaster meant the death of the golden goose, but a filmed
disaster could be recycled with bigger and bigger profits each time, since
audiences knew in advance that their macabre hopes would be fulfilled.
By 1915 Glenn Martin, was receiving $700.00, a handsome sum in that
era, for his stuntflying in the film *The Girl from Yesterday*, featuring
Mary Pickford.[16] That producers could pay Martin so well is an
indication that these action-packed feature films were prospering at the
movie box office, just as melodrama had prospered on the legitimate
stage the century before.

The story lines were eventually integrated into serials, later known
as cliff-hangers, a technique still utilized in today's soap opera format.
A cliff-hanger requires ending the action of the story during a
breathtaking moment, and having it resume in the next segment. This
technique originated in the *Chicago Tribune* (1913) where it was

successfully introduced to increase the sale of newspapers, which were purchased by readers eager to find out what happened in the next installment.[17] Likewise it increased theatre and film box office ticket sales by people who wanted to know what happened to their heroine or hero.

As aerial action became more dangerous, the melodramatic heroine of the legitimate stage was transplanted, "replete with virtue intact," to the motion picture screen. Her first transplant came in 1914 with the serial the *Perils of Pauline*, featuring Pearl White. As a former stunt-woman, White was familiar with the thrills that could be squeezed out of the fragile and chaste alabaster lady facing consummate evil. Perhaps it was her awareness of the popularity of such a contrast which dictated that she play "opposite a Curtiss Pusher biplane for several episodes."[18] Other films featuring heroines and airplanes sometimes together were *Sky Ranger* (Pathé, 1921) with June Caprice and *The Timber Queen* (Pathé, 1922) with Ruth Roland. Films featuring aerobatics included *Around the World in 18 Days* (Universal, 1923); and *The Eagle's Talons* (Universal, 1923).[19]

The making of films was temporarily interrupted, like so many other fledgling American institutions, by World War I in 1917. But as the list above demonstrates, when the war ended, filmmakers returned with more vigor to the production of aviation films. The increasing portrayal of aviation was fueled by a by-product of the war, a surplus of military airplanes. These produced a flurry of purchases by anyone who had $300.00 to $600.00, the going price for a Curtiss Jenny still in its crate. White women who had the money, as well as white men, purchased airplanes and began to appear as stuntflyers, both in live barnstorming acts and in feature films during the mid-twenties. So the barnstormers flew, and the movie cameras rolled and both profited-- with the movie producers having less to risk, of course.

By the time Coleman forwarded her letter to Norman Studios, feature films had become a permanent attraction in the vaudeville houses. At least two were subjects of popular celluloid entertainment: German World War I ace Manfred von Richthofen, the subject of a popular German produced, fictionalized biographical film (*Richthofen*, 1921); and French ace Captain Charles Nungesser, who piloted the stuntplane in the 1925 American produced film *Sky Raiders*. Coleman was well-known in the African American communities, not only through the newspapers, but from her newsreels shown in African American theatres. Of these newsreels and her popularity, she wrote with confidence to Richard Norman in the February 3 letter mentioned above: "I know I have been a success in every house I have played in Chicago and other cities. And with only 2 reels [newsreels] as an added attraction."[20] It was an auspicious moment for Coleman's entrance into feature films, and she knew it.

Stuntflying in films had become a lucrative occupation for white men and white women. Coleman decided to appeal to Richard Norman, a white man who had established his film career as an independent director by featuring positive images of African Americans on screen. By appealing to him then, Coleman once again reinforced her concern for maintaining a positive image of African Americans, while at the same time attempting to use the prestige of her own image to do so.

Richard Norman was likewise enthusiastic. He seemed genuinely moved by and supportive of Coleman's mission; but he also saw box-office dollar signs. Before he and Coleman corresponded about a film featuring her life and work, this independent producer had been in touch with the man who was functioning as her booking agent at that time, a Mr. D. Ireland Thomas. Norman and Thomas had agreed that Coleman would perform the aerial stunts for the *The Flying Ace*, a film completed and released in 1926 after her death.[21] In a January 19, 1926 letter to D. Ireland Thomas, Richard Norman wrote that "There is no doubt that Miss Coleman would be a great drawing card in a 5 or 6 reel feature, featuring some of her flying."[22]

Coleman's response to Norman's overtures on *The Flying Ace* project rejected any chance that she would play a minor role. She was unwilling to relinquish artistic control. Not only, she wrote him, would she be willing to raise her own money to underwrite the cost of the film, but she had already written her own script entitled, "Yesterday, Today and Tomorrow." She felt assured that she would recover the investment of both time and money because, as she put it, "I am more than <u>Sure</u> [sic] my picture will go big in Colored houses I <u>know</u> [sic] this, as a Fact as my two News reels have drawn in house more so than some Colored Drama."[23]

In his reply to Coleman, Norman displays no signs of being intimidated by this strong-willed, self-confident woman. He reiterated his enthusiasm that any film that Coleman proposed and flew in would be a success. He also requested that she provide him with more detailed plans for the making of the film. Yet, Coleman's plans to use the film medium to reach and convince the African American community of the necessity for them to become involved in aviation was not to be. She crashed to her death two months later. Norman released *The Flying Ace* during the latter part of that year. He was consistent in featuring African Americans in positive imagery, and there is an airplane. But it remains on the ground. There are no aerial stunts, by Coleman or anyone else.

The effect of aerial stunts in the film Norman released are accomplished by careful shooting, juxtaposition, and editing. The year of Coleman's death, then, coincides with the time that film industry jumped from inescapable verity to illusion, to *tromp de l'oeil* (a French phrase meaning literally "trickery of the eye"). This increasing sophistication, however, must be accomplished by the loss of what is real, true, and solid. Just as Coleman's death predates by three years the stockmarket crash, the beginning of the Great Depression and the end of the New Negro Era, so too does Norman's release of this film mark the move away from Coleman's intent to use the medium as a forum for increased political awareness and activity, toward "pure" entertainment for the sake of escapism.

That Coleman entertained is not the source of her uniqueness. African Americans had established themselves as outstanding entertainers from their days on the plantations. Many entertained to save their lives and/or the lives of their loved ones by diverting the attention of the master. After Emancipation, many found that entertainment was the only avenue to employment, and in some cases, to real independence--they could determine when and if they would perform.

Coleman's uniqueness resides in the manner in which she manipulated entertainment in an airplane against all obstacles for her own intentions. Her cleverness in understanding and exploiting the cultural, the social, and the political practices of her era are admirable, although she lacked commensurate recognition. Coleman did not let racism or sexism deter her from her mission. She instead used this prejudice as a conduit to her goal. She exploited racism by becoming a staunch nationalist as a standard around which to rally African Americans. She exploited sexism by retaining a ladylike demeanor while entering the male realm of aviation.

Like her plantation slave predecessors, she diverted the masters' attention, while accomplishing what she wanted to do. This is not to imply that all of her actions were a reaction to the political climate, but that she forged a variation of her original agenda every time one of these institutions threatened to impede her objective. Thus she joined a continuum of the ranks of her ancestors who had transcended the limited parameters of the legitimate stage, while always keeping her "eye on the prize" for the betterment of the African American community.

Having worked in a men's barber shop, run with the entertainment crowd, established her own business, and survived the 1919 Chicago race riots, Coleman had her eyes and finger on the pulse of American society, culture, and politics. She knew both how to adapt to and control them. Coleman did nothing haphazardly; she was a selfless yet shrewd businesswoman whose timing of such undertakings indicate a kindred astuteness to P. T. Barnum and Tony Pastor. All of them knew what their audiences wanted and gave it to them, and all altered history in some way with their decisions.

Today when people mention women in aviation, Coleman's contemporary Amelia Earhart is the reflex response. Coleman and Earhart both had supportive and encouraging mothers. When Coleman's mother was nurturing her on Dunbar, Washington, and Tubman, Earhart's mother was nurturing her on Sewell and Potter. While

Earhart's childhood exposure to *Black Beauty* and *Peter Rabbit* developed the "crusader" for the underdog in her, and developed a lasting protective inclination which summoned her anger and propelled her into action for mistreated animals;[24] Coleman's exposure to Dunbar, and Washington, her observations of the malevolent treatment by white Americans of her family and other African Americans, as well as her personal experiences with white racism and bigotry more than developed her crusader spirit. Coleman's mother was working as a washerwoman, however, while Earhart's mother hired a washerwoman. Coleman's mother sent her to college from monies earned from washing and picking cotton, and the daughter had to drop out because her money ran out. Earhart, by comparison, was intermittently in and out of school because she could not determine what she wanted to major in. When Coleman wanted to fly, she had to go to France to learn and to receive an international license--only to be told that she could not purchase or fly an airplane in the United States.[25] When Earhart wanted to fly, her father gave her the money and she flew. When Coleman wanted an airplane, she had to have a white person purchase it for her. When Earhart wanted an airplane, her mother purchased it for her.[26] When Coleman was the butt of racism and sexism, she had to devise clever ways in which to circumvent them. When Earhart suffered the indignities of sexism, she co-founded the Ninety-Nines, comprised of other white aviatrixes. In order to continue to perform to raise money for an aviation school, Coleman had to continue to risk her life by flying in any airplane she could find, and by entrusting their mechanical welfare to unknown mechanics, a dependence that some of her admirers such as the Reverend Junius Caesar Austin, Sr. (see Chapter IV), and Ross D. Brown (see pp. xii-xiii), believed sent Coleman to an early death. Even Earhart recognized that loyal family and friends were essential to the prolongation of an aviator's life. Years later, concerning her mother's financial assistance in the purchase of her first aircraft Earhart wrote retrospectively that, "I didn't realize it at the time, but cooperation of one's family and close friends is one of the greatest safety factors a fledgling flyer can have."[27] When Earhart decided that she wanted aviation to be her life's work, she married George Palmer Putnam, the publisher. Eleanor Roosevelt entertained Earhart, and Miriam A. ("Ma") Ferguson, the first woman Governor in the United States, honored Bessie Coleman for her achievements. When Earhart determined not to make any more flights across the sea in a single-engine plane because it was too dangerous, Purdue University raised $50,000 for the Amelia Earhart Fund, to build a "flying laboratory" with dual engines; whereas Coleman met her death while on a lecture circuit attempting to raise funds from the African American sector of the South in order to establish an aviation school free of discrimination.

Both had relatively short-lived careers in aviation: Coleman began flying in 1921 and fatally crashed in 1926, an active career of only five years; and Earhart pursued aviation on a fulltime basis for only about ten years, concluding with her mysterious disappearance in 1937. But while Earhart lived in a society that indulged and nurtured her, that same society attempted to impede Coleman's every move. While that same society has kept Earhart's memory alive through books, photographs, posters and other popular paraphernalia, Coleman's memoirs had to be privately published by her sister Elois Patterson, who was turned down by several publishers because there was no interest in the story.[28] While yet another generation of Earhart worshippers continue to write books surmising what really happened to Earhart, there are those who, indeed, remember Coleman. The majority of these loyalists are African Americans, both women and men.

The late Janet Harmon Bragg (née Waterford), a registered nurse sounded the first call in an attempt to rally African Americans into aviation one year after Coleman's death. She stated in her newspaper column in 1927:

> Bessie Coleman, America's premiere woman aviator, has been dead a year. All America was shocked when last May her plane crashed down to earth at Jacksonville, Fla., bringing death to the most daring of American women. Since her death we have done little or nothing in the realm of aviation. Disaster seems to attend all our efforts in this field, partly because of a lack of interest on our part, and partly because of insufficient preparation on the part of those who are trying. We are barred from schools of aviation; the government shuts the doors of its air training departments in our faces, and lack of funds makes it impossible for us to procure first class equipment for our efforts in aviation.... Bessie Coleman was fortunate in receiving her training in Paris, but there is no reason why we should lose our interest in flying because of her tragic end. Rather, it should stimulate us to greater efforts to keep alive her name.[29]

Two years after Coleman's fatal crash, Atty. Oscar C. Brown, Chairman of the Board of Promotion for the Co-operative Business, Professional and Labor League of Cook County, Chicago; of which Reverend J.C. Austin was Executive Secretary forwarded a letter to The Honorable Herbert Hoover, then Secretary of Commerce in Washington, D.C. informing him of an upcoming memorial unveiling for Coleman.

Sir:

On the morning of May thirtieth, the colored citizens of
Chicago will unveil a monument which they are placing over
the grave of the late Bessie Coleman, a Negro aviatrix, who
lost her life on April thirtieth, 1926, when her plane fell from
a distance of 5,300 feet above the City of Jacksonville,
Florida.

To us there seems a great responsibility to be ever alert to
encourage Negro boys and girls in their life battles for success
and fame; and to keep alive the deeds of those who make
worthy contributions to our civilization's onward march.

This is the spirit that motivates our act in helping to
perpetuate the memory of this heroic and courageous aviatrix,
who, as a pioneer, gave her last full measure of devotion in
furtherance of the science of aviation.

A word of recognition and encouragement from you, as
Secretary of Commerce of Our Great Nation, would be highly
inspirational for the occasion; and for it we shall be very
grateful.

Very respectfully yours,
Oscar C. Brown
Chairman, Board of Promotion.[30]

The Assistant Secretary of Commerce immediately forwarded a nite
[sic] later, dated May 26, 1928 acknowledging Bessie Coleman and
expressing the importance of the planned unveiling:

It has come to my attention that you are unveiling a
monument in memory of Bessie Coleman stop [sic] I trust
that this monument will not only serve to commemorate her
achievements and sacrifices but also to stimulate others of her
race to high purposes and worthy accomplishments

Wm. P. MacCracken, Jr.
Assistant Secretary of Commerce for Aeronautics[31]

Thematically, both letters stress the necessity for acknowledging
Coleman as a role model to inspire future generations of African
Americans towards high achivement.

In 1929, William J. Powell was founder and president of the Bessie
Coleman Aero Clubs in Los Angeles established to keep Coleman's
dream alive by encouraging young African Americans to become
aviators. The Clubs provided aviation training and airplanes for student

training. James Herman Banning, a barnstormer, a transcontinental aviator, and the first African American to earn a license from the Department of Commerce (1926), was one of these students.[32] Further, in honor of Coleman, on Labor Day of 1931 the Bessie Coleman Aero Clubs sponsored the first all African American Air Show in the United States; there were 15,000 spectators present. William J. Powell operated The Bessie Coleman School which grew out of these clubs, where he continued to train African American Aviators on the West Coast throughout the Depression. Powell published his book, *Black Wings* in 1934, dedicated it to Bessie Coleman and included a frontispiece of her in full aviation attire.[33]

On the East Coast Robert Abbott and the National Urban League along with other organizations continued throughout the Depression to keep the interest in aviation alive in African American communities by sponsoring lecture tours and training programs designed with this intent. The Challenger Air Pilot's Association, a national organization of African American aviators, inspired by the legacy of Bessie Coleman, was founded in 1931. Although Chicago was its homebase, the Association constructed its first airstrip in the African American township of Robins, Illinois in 1933, because the Chicago airports were off-limits to African Americans.[34] During the same year, Charles Alfred "Chief" Anderson and Dr. Albert E. Forsythe (who also worked with the National Urban League in promoting aviation among African Americans), connected the East and West African American's aviation activities when they flew from Atlantic City to Los Angeles and back. It was the first transcontinental flight made by African Americans. In 1934, these two men honored the memory of Booker T. Washington when they received international acclaim for flying the Pan-American Goodwill Flight in their Lambert Monocoupe, dubbed the "Spirit of Booker T. Washington." This flight covered Miami, Nassau, Havana, Jamaica, Haiti, the Dominican Republic, Puerto Rico, the Virgin Islands, Grenada, Trinidad, and British Guiana; its purpose was to promote interracial harmony and demonstrate the developing prowess of African American aviators.[35]

The exploits of Bessie Coleman were again penned in 1935 and 1936. Ross D. Brown pays homage to Bessie Coleman in a poem bearing her name, published in his second edition of *Watching My Race Go By: Feats, Facts, and Faults of the Negro Race* in 1935. the late Janet Harmon Bragg (née Waterford), had herself become a stuntflying aviatrix by the time she again wrote of Coleman's contributions to aviation in her column the "Negro in Aviation," a weekly section of *The Chicago Defender* in 1936. Although this section was developed to report on the activities of Col. John C. Robinson, an African American aviator who was then in charge of the Imperial Ethiopian Air Forces in Addis Ababa under the rule of Emperor Haile Selassie, Bragg would not

let her readers forget that it was Bessie Coleman who inspired the race
to engage in aviation. Under the heading "Race Interest In Aviation In
Actuality Begins With Advent of Bessie Coleman" she wrote that,

> Brave Bess strove untiringly to interest members of the Race
> in flying; to become airminded. She told them, way back
> when, that aviation was America's coming industry and that
> someday as the business of flying increased and became more
> practical, a place would have to be found for them. ...Brave
> Bess did not die in vain! It did more than any other single
> event to spur young men and women to seek knowledge of
> aviation.
> There developed a strong desire on the part of young people to
> obtain information about aviation from the ground up. It
> appears that the death of the lovable Miss Coleman encouraged
> men and women to learn about flying so as to prevent a
> recurrence of such tragedies. They set out enthusiastically to
> help conquer the airlanes to avenge the death of that splendid
> little flyer.[36]

Bragg along with Willa Brown, Cornelius Coffey, and Dale White
were among a group of Black pilots who flew a memorial flight over
Coleman's grave in 1935, a commemoration for Coleman that
continues today. Dorothy Darby, a noted parachutist also inspired by
Coleman's valor, received her pilots license in May 1938, and honored
Coleman by flying over her grave during Memorial Day Ceremonies
the same year.[37] In June 1938, Willa Brown who had begun her
training in aviation under the instruction of Dorothy Darby, and Col.
John C. Robinson, received her private pilot's license with a score of
96%, the highest grade ever received by an African American woman,
and one which permitted her to carry passengers.[38]

Brown following Coleman's example, also enlisted the assistance
of *The Chicago Defender* Editor, Robert Abbott when she embarked
upon her career in aviation.[39] During the early 1930s Abbott was
financially sponsoring tours of African American aviators to African
American colleges and universities for the purpose of encouraging the
youth there to get involved in aviation and lobbying Congress to
include African Americans in federally sponsored aviation programs.
Brown, however, completed her training at the Coffey School of
Aeronautics, founded by Cornelius R. Coffey and John C. Robinson
who had graduated from Chicago's Curtiss Wright School of
Aeronautics in 1928. Both were initially denied admission because of
their race, but the school relented after both educated men, and employed
automobile mechanics, threatened the Wright School with a lawsuit

endorsed by their employer, Emil Mack, President of Elmwood Park Motors. In spite of relentless harassment Coffey and Robinson graduated with distinction in 1928, after which the school enlisted them as instructors with a mandate that they recruit African Americans. With the assistance of *The Chicago Defender* and *The Pittsburgh Courier,* they successfully recruited thirty-two African Americans.[40] Janet Harmon Bragg (née Waterford) was one of the five women in this segregated class.

In 1939, Dale White and Chauncey E. Spencer (son of Anne Spencer, poet and Virginia's literary salon queen of the Harlem Renaissance), flew to Washington and lobbied Congress to provide contracts for the government Civilian Pilots Training Program for the training of African Americans.[41] Their trip climaxed in an unexpected conference with Senator Harry S. Truman, to whom they disclosed that African Americans where excluded from both this program, and all military air services. Truman who was unaware of this exclusion stated upon viewing White and Spencer's airplane, "... if you had guts enough to fly this thing to Washington... I've got guts enough to see that you get what you are asking for."[42]

This fortuitous meeting was instrumental in yielding contracts for the Coffey School of Aeronautics located at the Harlem Airport in Chicago and at this time operated by Willa Brown and Cornelius R. Coffey. In addition to training some of the most celebrated African American Pilots of WW II (several went on to become members of the celebrated Tuskeegee Airmen) under the government Civilian Pilots Training Program, together they paved the way for integration of the aviation industry as they trained both African and white American pilots. Brown became the first African American Officer in the Civil Air Patrol, a member of the Federal Aviation Administration's (FAA) Women's Advisory Board, and by 1943, she was the only woman in the United States concurrently holding a mechanic's license, a commercial license, and functioning as president of a large Aviation Corporation.[43] As President of the United States, Harry S. Truman terminated segregation in the armed forces by endorsing Executive Order 9981 on July 26, 1948.[44] Although this decision was a victory for African Americans in the Armed Forces, additional measures had to be undertaken in order to achieve equity for African Americans in the social and cultural spheres of the United States. As the late Enoch P. Waters notes:

> Truman's order was the first since Lincoln's Emancipation Proclamation that had a favorable effect on the lives of millions of blacks [sic]. Between the two, there had been a number of court decisions affecting Negro rights. While each was another nail in the coffin of ole jim crow, they were

important only to small segments of the race: students in publicly supported professional schools, interstate bus and Pullman passengers, those who wanted to purchase homes in white neighborhoods, defendants in criminal trials and users of public libraries. But because every male citizen, 18 years and older, was subject to the military draft, this order affected the lives of millions of young black men.[45]

Progress towards the disintegration of segregation in the civilian sector of the United States was not to begin until 1954 with the Supreme Court decision in *Brown v. The Board of Education of Topeka* which rendered racially segregated schools unconstitutional. This ruling overturned the 1896 *Plessy v. Ferguson* decision that made separate but equal facilities lawful.

Commemorative flights for Bessie Coleman were kept alive by the Challenger Air Pilot's Association from the 1930s until the late 1960s. This commemorative activity lay dormant for a short period as the pilots began to retire. The Bessie Coleman Aviators a contemporary organization of young African American women pilots made the flight again on April 30, 1975. On April 30, 1980 Rufus Hunt, aviation historian and pilot revived the practice as an annual affair of flying low and dropping a wreath of flowers on Coleman's grave at Lincoln Cemetery in Southwest Chicago. He has continued to organize several pilots annually, and in April 1989, a record number of aviators including white pilots paid tribute to Coleman in this manner.[46]

Today, there are engraved granite plaques next to two trees located in Atchison, Kansas--Earhart's birthplace. Each plaque is engraved with a name--one with Bessie Coleman, the other with Amelia Earhart--representing them in The International Forest of Friendship and commemorating their "exceptional contributions to aviation."[47] The forest was a bicentennial gift to the United States from The International Ninety-Nines (1929), an organization of women pilots, of which Earhart was co-founder, and the first president. The forest features trees from the fifty states, territories and the forty-one countries representing the location of more than 6000 members worldwide. On special occasions a representative flag is flown next to each tree.

Ida Van Smith, instrument rated aviatrix (can fly in inclement weather solely by reading the instrument panel), member of the Ninety-Nines, certified ground instructor, recipient of the Bishop Wright Aviation Award, and founder of the twenty-two year old Ida Van Smith Flight Clubs for ages 3-19, has carried on Bessie Coleman's dream.[48] Her clubs have educated several hundred students nationally in aviation, most of them African Americans. Smith sponsored the inauguration of Coleman to the International Forest of Friendship on July 19, 1986. With the resurgence of the popularity of air shows nationally and internationally, it is only just that Coleman's granite plaque is finally among those of other people who are considered pioneers in aviation, many of whom began as barnstormers. People such as Jimmy Dolittle, (awarded the 1989 Presidential Medal by President George Bush); Charles Lindbergh, Howard Hughes; Anne Morrow Lindbergh, and Dwight D. Eisenhower (America's only pilot president), among others, are recognized here.

The 1920s was an opportune decade for Bessie Coleman as an African American woman whose prerequisites for aspiring pilots were courage, nerve, ambition to fly and the volition to dare death.[49] Women had fought for and attained their political right to vote. The African American intelligentsia was becoming a force to be reckoned with through artistic, literary, and business endeavors. African American women were in the vanguard of political, social and cultural activities. The Harlem Renaissance was the ideal backdrop for Coleman to further exploit the genius of African American entertainment in an effort that would eventually alter history for American society, in World War II, and all wars thereafter. Coleman's life may have influenced Josephine Baker who later said that she expatriated to France because:

> One day I realized I was living in a country where I was afraid to be black. It was only a country for white people, not black, so I left. I had been suffocating in the United States. I can't live anywhere that I can't breathe freedom.... Haven't I that right? I was created free. No chains did I wear when I came here. A lot of us left, not because we wanted to leave, but because we couldn't stand it anymore. Branded, banded, cut off. Canada Lee, Dr. Dubois [sic], Paul Robeson, Marcus Garvey-- all of us, forced to leave.[50]

Baker, who had club-hopped with Coleman during her youth, later refused to perform in nightclubs unless African Americans were admitted, just as Coleman had refused in Waxahachie, Texas and in Orlando, Florida during her scheduled aerial exhibitions.

It is clear that Coleman was prepared to develop her life story for popular entertainment and that she had no delusions of her self-worth in such an endeavor. All who have spoken of Coleman use adjectives such as unselfish, in control, determined, beautiful, and strong-willed. All seem to agree that there was no selfish or personal ulterior motive for her drive to build a school for other African Americans. Coleman selflessly forged ahead beyond racism, sexism and material limits for the advancement of all African Americans. She joined the continuum of African Americans who contributed positively to the political climate and cultural improvement of her race people. She had an exemplary character and was admired by young and old, Black and white, rich and poor. Coleman was always conscious that she was presenting an image of the entire race in her endeavors. The following letter, found in the pocket of her jacket after her fatal crash, exemplifies the esteem in which she was held even by a younger generation of African Americans:

> Mrs.Coleman,
> My Dear One: I am writing you to congratulate you on your brave doings. I want to be an aviatrix when I get a woman. I like to see our own Race do brave things. I am going to be out there to see you jump from the airplane. I want an airplane of my own when I get a woman. Many kisses.
>
> Yours a little girl,
RUBY MAE McDUFFIE[51]

Coleman reflected this atmosphere in her decision to become an aviatrix. Although she was part Choctaw and African American, she identified Black (in the pan-African sense), expressing racial consciousness and pride in her drive to build an aviation school for African Americans. She exercised political savvy by attending the Pan African Conference in France, and through continued association with Garveyites. When it was suggested that she "pass," she would take her darker complexioned mother, or more frequently her niece Marion Coleman with her during business meetings to emphasize that she was indeed Black.

Some African Americans did indeed "pass" for white, or at least American Indian. But Coleman's Black-identified stance, in historical context, was an open rebellion against the social restrictions collectively known as "Jim Crow," the laws and codes of social conduct that mandated complete segregation by race. Such restrictions were sometimes designated and enforced by law, and many times by extralegal means utilized by vigilante groups. Whether legal or not, these restrictions were designed to exclude African Americans from mainstream American life. Not all white Americans agreed with the goal that America move as quickly to full integration as possible. But while a few did work actively for an egalitarian society, the majority of the public was silent, and in some cases apathetic.

Nevertheless, a cruel irony underlies this general public acceptance of "Jim Crow." On the one hand, American laws and customs locked African Americans out of virtually all routes to equal opportunities through employment, education, and access to public facilities. But on the other hand, the popular self-image which most Americans held of their nation was that of an expansively pluralistic society, capable of absorbing and transforming multitudes of diverse cultures into a coherent, distinctively American culture. Waves upon waves of European immigrants availed themselves of American resources, and prospered according to their efforts. The contrast between the image of America for European immigrants and for African Americans was striking:

> America as the refuge of huddled masses yearning to be free; America as a domain of boundless frontier; America as freedom's dream castle--these are the components of the white culture theorizer's perspective. The black perspective is another thing altogether. The masses are huddled in dark holds; the domain is one of endless slavery; and the domicile is one of bigotry's major fortresses. The cultures that proceed out of these differing perspectives are polarized, and the bodies of intellectual and imaginative work that reflect these different cultures--while their artistic forms merge at times--stand in striking contrast to one another.[52]

The difference in perspective between the two groups necessarily created a difference in the form and function of art by each. Generally speaking, art by and for European immigrants could afford to function as escapist entertainment, because social and economic progress was available to them through other avenues, including business, industry and education. Further, European artistic production mirrored aesthetic and structural components with which its audience was already familiar, and thus comfortable. Americanization of such art could and did proceed gradually.

African Americans, on the other hand, did not have the luxury of producing art primarily for other African Americans. They could not afford to draw upon a limited segment of the population for their audiences. Entertainment was one of the few areas in which economic success was possible, and with that economic success some measure of inclusion and acceptance in American society. As a result, African American artistic production draws upon aesthetic and structural components which are familiar to a wide range of audiences, in order to appeal to as many potential audience members as possible. Coleman's use of barnstorming is one example of this kind of reliance on familiar components. However, African American artistic production also tends to introduce ingenious new changes or twists in conventional forms, in order to attract as large an audience as possible through an appeal to curiosity and novelty. Artistic production, then, is one of the most important institutions in which African Americans have sought to attain what is commonly referred to as the "American Dream." They have developed new areas in American entertainment and augmented those already in existence.

Bessie Coleman's innovations as a Black woman are an especially significant contribution to the development of new artistic forms. Historically, Black women have encountered discrimination not only based on race, but on gender as well. During slavery, they were valued as breeders of slaves, rather than as contributors to the intellectual and social building of America. Even after the end of enslavement, they have had to continue to struggle to define their own existence and "place" in American society beyond the circumscription of reproduction.

Bessie Coleman provided an alternative form of entertainment for all Americans, Black and white. In so doing, she demonstrated that a Black woman was capable of thoughtful and innovative contributions to American popular culture. She demonstrated that occupations for African American men and women need not be limited to menial labor, within an environment of exploitation and degradation. Finally, she used an entertainment vehicle to inspire all African Americans to continue their proud struggle against segregation and discrimination in all forms, and to continue working toward full, productive citizenship in America.

Notes

1. "Aviatrix Must Sign Away Life To Learn Trade," *Chicago Defender* 8 October 1921: 2.

2. "Harlem's Newest Apartments Named After Black 'Joan of Arc,'" *The New York News*, 23 July 1927: N. pag.; and "The Monument to Bessie Coleman," 30 July 1927: N. pag. Note: Joan of Arc has been immortalized in theatre by Shakespeare in *Henry VI* (1590-1592); by Voltaire in La Pucelle (1755); by Schiller in *Die Jungfrau von Orleans* (1801); by George Bernard Shaw in *Saint Joan* (1923); and by Jean Anouilh's *L'Alouette* (1953), translated by Christopher Fry as The Lark (1955).

3. "Bessie to Fly Over Gotham: Queen Bess to Ride Air Next Sunday," *Chicago Defender* 26 August 1922: 1; "Texas Negro Girl Becomes Able Aviatrix," *Houston Post Dispatch* 7 May 1925: 4.

4. "Here Soon!: Aviatrix Bessie Coleman," Advertisement Flyer, c. 1923.

5. My inquiries in 1985 of all of the film houses that hold 1920s films and newsreels were unfruitful. These houses include Pathe Pictures; Sherman Grinberg Film Library, Inc./East and West Coast Offices; RKO Pictures; University of South Carolina who in March of 1980 had received several million feet of Movietonews film from Twentieth Century-Fox Film Corporation. Several of the experts from these establishments believe that the film may have chemically disintegrated in the "can" as so much of the film of that period has.

6J. James H. Farmer, *Celluloid Wings: The Impact of Movies on Aviation* (Pennsylvania: Tab Books Inc., 1984) 7.

7. Elois Coleman Patterson, *Memoirs of the Late Bessie Coleman Aviatrix:* Pioneer of the Negro People in Aviation (Elois Patterson, 1969) N. pag.

8. Letter from Bessie Coleman to Norman Studios, in the Black Film Center Archive, Indiana University, Bloomington. Courtesy of Professor Phyllis R. Klotman, Director. The letter is dated at "Tampa, Fla, 3rd February, 1926."

9. Farmer 2-3.

10. Thomas Cripps, *Slow Fade to Black: The Negro in American Film, 1900-1942* (New York: Oxford University Press, 1977) 12.

11. For actual titles, dates, studios, and producers see Phyllis Rauch Klotman, *Frame by Frame: A Black Filmography* (Indiana University Press, 1979); James Weldon Johnson writes in *Black Manhattan* that, Sam Lucas, the "Grand Old Man" of the Negro stage, was the first Black person to portray Uncle Tom in the film version of *Uncle Tom's Cabin* (1915), 90-91.

12. Farmer 3.

13. Farmer 6.

14. Farmer 7.

15. Farmer 8; Roger E. Bilstein, "Symbolism and Imagery," *Flight Patterns: Trends of Aeronautical Development in the United States, 1918-1929* (Athens: The University of Georgia Press, 1983) 150.

16. Farmer 9.

17. Terry Ramsaye, "The Screen and Press Conspire," *A Million and One Nights: A History of the Motion Picture* (New York: Simon and Schuster, 1964) 652-669. This chapter provides a comprehensive description of how the *Chicago Tribune* developed the newspaper serial *The Adventures of Kathlyn*, and syndicated it to Selig pictures through the General Film Company to run simultaneously on the movie screen.

18. Farmer 10.

19. Farmer 10.

20. Letter from Bessie Coleman to Norman Studios, in the Black Film Center Archive, Indiana University, Bloomington. Courtesy of Professor Phyllis R. Klotman, Director. The letter is dated at "Tampa, Fla, 3rd February, 1926."

21. There is a copy of *The Flying Ace* housed in the Black Film Center Archive, Indiana University, Bloomington.

22. Letter from Richard Norman to Mr. D. Ireland Thomas, Charleston, S. C., in the Black Film Center Archive, Indiana University, Bloomington. Courtesy of Professor Phyllis R. Klotman, Director. The letter is dated at N.p. "19th January, 1926."

23. Letter from Bessie Coleman to Norman Studios, in the Black Film Center Archive, Indiana University, Bloomington. Courtesy of Professor Phyllis R. Klotman, Director. The letter is dated at "W. Palm Beach, Fla, 23rd February, 1926."

24. Muriel Earhart Morrissey and Carol L. Osborne, *Amelia, My Sister: Biography of Amelia Earhart, True Facts About Her Disappearance* (California: Osborne Publisher, Incorporated, 1987) 20.

25. Judy Lomax, "Amelia Earhart: America's Winged Legend," *Women of the Air* (New York: Dodd, Mead & Company, 1987) 68.

26. Lomax 69.

27. Amelia Earhart, *The Fun of It: Random Records of My Own Flying and of Women in Aviation* (Chicago: Academy Press Limited, 1977) 27.

28. Marion Coleman, personal interview with Elizabeth Hadley Freydberg and Kathleen Collins, 12 January 1985; Dean Stallworth, telephone interview with Elizabeth Hadley Freydberg 24 October 1984.

29. "Bessie Coleman," *Chicago Defender* 14 March 1927: 2.

30. Letter from Oscar C. Brown to The Honorable Herbert Hoover, Secretary of Commerce, Washington, D.C. The letter is dated at

"Chicago, Illinois, 21st May, 1928." Record Group 237, Federal Aviation Administration, Central Files. National Archives and Records Administration: Washington, DC.

31. Nite [sic] Letter from Wm. P. MacCracken, Jr., Assistant Secretary of Commerce for Aeronautics to Oscar C. Brown, Cooperative Business, Professional and Labor League, 3301 Indiana Avenue, Chicago, Illinois. The letter is dated at "Washington, D.C., 26th May 1928." Record Group 237, Federal Aviation Administration, Central Files. National Archives and Records Administration: Washington, DC.

32. "Flying Free: Early Black Aviators Break the Color Barrier." *Paine: A Magazine for Alumni and Friends of the College.* Autumn 1986: 2+.

33. See William J. Powell, *Black Wings* (Los Angeles: Ivan Deach Publishing Company, 1934) an excellent personal narrative of the opposition Powell, although college educated, endured during his attempt to become an aviator because he was an African American; and of the trials and tribulations of establishing an aviation school for African Americans.

34. Von Hardesty and Dominick Pisano, *Black Wings: The American Black in Aviation* (Washington, D.C.: National Air And Space Museum, 1983) 12.

35. Von Hardesty and Pisano, 16-17.

36. Janet Harmon Waterford (Bragg), "Race Interest In Aviation In Actuality Begins With Advent of Bessie Coleman," *Chicago Defender* 28 March 1936:1.

37. "Granted Pilots License [Dorothy Darby, Parachute Jumper]," *Chicago Defender* 21 May 1938: 1.

38. "Young Aviatrix To Teach Air-Minded Billikens The Principles of Aviation," *Chicago Defender* 16 May 1936:15; "Young Woman Flyer Gets Pilots License: Willa Brown, Chicago Aviatrix, Can Carry Passengers, Give Instructions or Make Cross-Country Flights," *Pittsburgh Courier* 2 July 1938: 11+.

39. Enoch P. Waters, "Little Air Show Becomes A National Crusade," *American Diary: A Personal History of the Black Press* (Chicago: Path Press, Inc., 1987) 195-197.

40. Rufus A. Hunt, *The Coffey Intersection* (Chicago: J.R.D.B. Enterprises, 1982) 21.

41. For a detailed account of Spencer's career in aviation, see Chauncey E. Spencer, *Who Is Chauncey Spencer?* (Detroit: Broadside Press, 1975); Von Hardesty and Dominick Pisano, *Black Wings: The American Black in Aviation* (Washington, D.C.: National Air and Space Museum, Smithsonian Institution, 1983) 20.

42. Kriz, Marjorie, "The Had Another Dream: Blacks Took to the Air Early," *U. S. Department of Transportation News*, reprinted from *FAA World*, January 1980. N. Pag.; Enoch P. Waters, "Little Air Show Becomes A National Crusade," *American Diary: A Personal History of the Black Press* (Chicago: Path Press, Inc., 1987) 206.

43. Karl E. Downs, "Willa B. Brown: Vivacious Aviatrix," *Meet the Negro* (Pasadena, CA: The Login Press, 1943) 54-55.

44. Von Hardesty and Dominick Pisano, *Black Wings: The American Black in Aviation* (Washington, D.C.: National Air and Space Museum, Smithsonian Institution, 1983) 57; Enoch P. Waters, "Little Air Show Becomes A National Crusade," *American Diary: A Personal History of the Black Press* (Chicago: Path Press, Inc., 1987) 209.

45.. Waters 210.

46. Harold Hurd, telephone conversation with Elizabeth Hadley Freydberg upon his return from the event 2 May 1989.

47. Copy of the Official Commemoration Certificate from The International Forest Of Friendship, July 19, 1986. The official seal of the City of Atchison, Kansas and signed by Dodie Emery, Mayor, City of Atchison; Fay Gilli Walls, Co-Chairman; and Joe Carriyan, Co-Chairman. Courtesy of Ida Van Smith, aviatrix and founder of the Ida Van Smith Flight Clubs.

48. Barbara-Marie Green, "Bessie Coleman First Black Aviatrix--A 'Woman With A Dream,'" *New York Voice* 20 October 1984: 13.

49. "Aviatrix Must Sign Away Life To Learn Trade," *Chicago Defender* 8 October 1921: 2.

50. Josephine Baker, "An Interview with Josephine Baker and James Baldwin," by Henry Louis Gates, Jr., James Olney, ed., *Afro-American Writing Today* (Louisiana: Louisiana State University Press, 1985) 11.

51. Letter from Ruby Mae McDuffie to Bessie Coleman. Appears in Evangeline Roberts, "Chicago Pays Parting Tribute to 'Brave Bessie' Coleman," *Chicago Defender* 15 May 1926: 2. The letter is dated at "Jacksonville, Fla, 29th April, 1926."

52. Houston A. Baker, Jr., "Completely Well: One View of Black American Culture," *Key Issues in the Afro-American Experience*, eds. Nathan I. Huggins, Martin Kilson, and Daniel M. Fox, vol. 1 (New York: Harcourt Brace Jovanovich, Inc., 1971) 27.

APPENDIX

Tampa Fla
Feb 3, 1926
Norman Studios
Arlington. Florida

Dear Sirs: —
I was given your address
by Mr. Trumbull owner
of The Liberty Theatre
St. Petersburg after
I appeared there in person
and on the screen with
2 reels showing my flights
in Europe & America

1. Letter from Bessie Coleman to Norman Studios, in the Black Film Center Archive, Indiana University, Bloomington. Courtesy of Professor Phyllis R. Klotman, Director. The letter is dated at "Tampa, Fla, 3rd February, 1926."

I have my life. work that I want put into pictures I know I have been a success in every house I have played in Chicago and other cities. And with only 2w as an added attraction I have titled my play Yesterday – Today & Tomorrow

If you are enerested which I am sure a few remarks from Mr. Trumbull will give you the correct idea what I will mean to you. and as any intelegent colored person know that I am the worlds first Col Flyer. man or woman. we have one Man now a Pilot 9 months

3.
in Tulsa if you are
enerested I will be willing
to go father into the matter
with you. I am, and know
it, the most known colored
person (woman alive)
other than the Jazz singers)

write me what you
would like to do about
this matter

            Bessie Coleman
            %. 1313 Marion St
            Tampa Fla.

W. Palm Beach Fla
Feb, 23, 1926

My Dear Mr. Norman
I just rec' your
letter it was Not fowared to
me as it should have been
yes Mr Norman I am More.
Than _Sure_ my picture will
go big in Colored houses
I know This, as a Fact as
my two News reels have
drawn in house more so
Than some Colored Drames

2. Letter from Bessie Coleman to Norman Studios, in the Black Film Center Archive, Indiana University, Bloomington. Courtesy of Professor Phyllis R. Klotman, Director. The letter is dated at "W. Palm Beach, Fla, 23rd February, 1926."

you may know what a real
Film of 5 reels would mean
you only have to ask the Mgr
at some of the Theatre in Fla
Tampa was not advertized
"at all" But in St. Petersburg
it was impossible to show that
Have a chance to return.
the picture that I want Filmed
maybe we could get together on
it, yesterday, To day and tomorrow
It would be better if we jointly
put out the photo as I am not
able to produce it independently
now if you are interested let
me know also give me a price
on directing 5 reels and let me hear
Bessie Coleman 530 First St

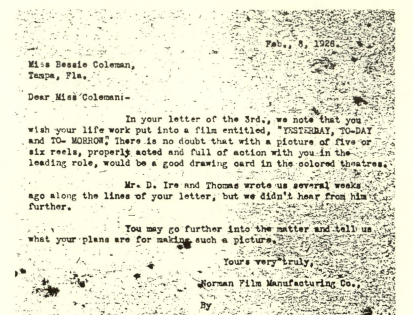

3. Letter from Richard Norman to Mr. D. Ireland Thomas, Charleston, S. C., in the Black Film Center Archive, Indiana University, Bloomington. Courtesy of Professor Phyllis R. Klotman, Director. The letter is dated at N.p. "19th January, 1926."

Jan., 19, 1926.

Mr. D. Ireland Thomas,
Charleston, S. C.

Dear Sir:-

Your letter of the 15th., in regard to Miss. Coleman, received.

There is no doubt that Miss Coleman would be a great drawing card in a 5 or 6 reel feature, featuring some of her flying, and I thank you for advising me of the opportunity to secure her for a picture.

I am just starting on a new picture called "The Flying Ace," in which there are many thrilling airplane stunts, therefore am equipped to supply all props Miss. Coleman would require for a picture.

I would suggest you interest someone to finance Miss Coleman in a picture, which I could make here very reasonable. For my part, I will say that I wouldn't care to undertake the financing of a picture for her as I am up to my neck in production in my own interest.

It will cost between four and five thousand dollars to make the proper kind of picture for her, and one which will bring the biggest returns. I find that colored audiences are becoming more critical, especially North, and more money must be spent in production than here-to-fore, and I can safely say that she can make a picture here for that amount which would cost her double or treble that amount, if the class of quality the same class of picture I can turn out here with my facilities.

Wishing you continued success with Miss Coleman and with best personal regards, I am,

Yours very truly,

4. Letter from Norman Film Manufacturing Co. to Miss Bessie Coleman, Tampa, Fla. in the Black Film Center Archive, Indiana University, Bloomington. Courtesy of Professor Phyllis R. Klotman, Director. The letter is dated at N.p. "8 Feb, 1926."

BIBLIOGRAPHY

"American Birdwomen," *Good Housekeeping*, 55:315-6; September 1912.

Anderson, Jervis. *This Was Harlem: A Cultural Portrait: 1900-1950.* New York: Farrar Straus Giroux, 1981.

Archer, Leonard C. *Black Images in the American Theatre: NAACP Protest Campaigns--Stage, Screen Radio & Television.* New York: Pageant-Poseidon, Ltd., 1973.

"Armed Services Integration," *Crisis,* July 1950: 443.

"Aviatrix Killed By Fall: Bessie Coleman and White Pilot in 2000 Ft. Crash." *The New York Amsterdam News* 5 May 1926: 1.

"Aviatrix Must Sign Away Life To Learn Trade." *The Chicago Defender* 8 October 1921: 2.

"Aviatrix to Fly at Driving Park." *Columbus Dispatch* 2 September 1923: 2.

Baker, Houston A. Jr. "Completely Well: One View of Black American Culture." *Key Issues in the Afro-American Experience.* Eds. Nathan I. Huggins, Martin Kilson and Daniel M. Fox. Vol. 1. New York: Harcourt Brace Jovanovich, Inc., 1971. 20-35. 2 vols.

Barbeau, Arthur E. and Florette Henri. "Two Black Fighting Outfits." *The Unknown Soldiers: Black American Troops in World War I.* Philadelphia: Temple University Press, 1974. 70-88.

Bardolph, Richard. *The Negro Vanguard.* Connecticut: Negro Universities Press, 1959.

Barr, Alwyn. *Black Texans: A History of Negroes in Texas 1528-1971.* Texas: Jenkins Publishing Company, The Pemberton Press, 1973.

"Bessie Coleman." *The Chicago Defender* 14 March 1927, 2: 2.

"Bessie Coleman Shows 'Em How." *The Afro-American* 8 September 1922: 1.

"Bessie Coleman The Race's Only Aviatrix Will Make Her Initial Local Flight At Checkerboard Airdrome Sunday, Oct. 15." *The Chicago Defender* 14 October 1922: 3.

"Bessie Gets Away; Does Her Stuff." *The Chicago Defender* 9 September 1922: 3.

"Bessie to Fly Over Gotham: Queen Bess to Ride Air Next Sunday." *The Chicago Defender* 26 August 1922: 1.

135

Bilstein, Roger E. *Flight Patterns: Trends of Aeronautical Development in the United States, 1918-1929.* Athens: The University of Georgia Press, 1983.

Bilstein, Roger and Jay Miller. "Men, Myths, and Machines: Early Civil Aviation and Its Legacy." *Aviation in Texas.* Texas: Texas Monthly Press, 1985. 7-15.

"Bird Woman Arrives," *The Afro-American* 18 August 1922: 10.

"'Bird' Woman Falls 2,000 Feet To Death," *The Afro-American* 8 May 1926: 1.

"Body of Bird Girl On Way to Chicago: Funeral to Be Held Friday Morning" 31 May 1926, unidentified newsclipping, in "Black Aviators" File, Schomburg Center Clipping File, New York Public Library.

Bogle, Donald. *Brown Sugar: Eighty Years of America's Black Female Superstars.* New York: Harmony Books, 1980.

Bolcom, Robert and William Kimball. *Reminiscing with Sissle and Blake.* New York: The Viking Press, 1973.

Bontemps, Arna and Jack Conroy. *Anyplace But Here.* 1945, Originally published as *They Seek a City.* New York: Hill and Wang, 1966.

"Brave Bessie: First Black Pilot in U. S. Was A Lady." *FAA General Aviation News*, January-February 1983: 17.

Brockett, Oscar. *The Theatre: An Introduction*, Historical Edition. 1964; Chicago: Holt, Rinehart, and Winston, Inc., 1979.

---. *World Drama.* New York: Holt, Rinehart, and Winston, Inc., 1984.

Bronson, Edgar Beecher. "An Aerial Bivouac." *Early Flight: From Balloons to Biplanes.* Ed. Frank Oppel. New Jersey: Castle, 1987. 188-196.

Brooks-Pazmany, Kathleen. *United States Women in Aviation 1919-1929.* City of Washington: Smithsonian Institution Press, 1983. (Smithsonian Studies in Air and Space, Number 5.)

Brown, Oscar C. Letter to The Honorable Herbert Hoover, Secretary of Commerce, Washington, D.C. 21 May 1928. Record Group 237, Federal Aviation Administration, Central Files. National Archives and Records Administration: Washington, DC.

Brown, Ross D. *Watching My Race Go By.* Chicago: R. D. Brown, 1935.

Buntin, Vera. Telephone interview with Elizabeth Hadley Freydberg and Kathleen Collins 12 January 1985.

Burkett, Randall K. "The Baptist Church in the Years of Crisis: J.C. Austin and Pilgrim Baptist Church, 1926-50." Unpublished essay, presented at a joint session of the American Society of Church History and the American Historical Association, the Northeast Seminar on Black Religion, and Religion and Society Series, University of Utah. By permission of Randall K. Burkett, W.E.B.

DuBois Institute for Afro-American Research, Harvard University, c. 1991.

Calbert, Jack Lynn. "James Edward and Miriam Amanda Ferguson: The 'Ma' and 'Pa' of Texas Politics." Diss. Indiana University/Bloomington, 1968.

Calloway, Cab and Bryant Rollins. *Of Minnie the Moocher and Me.* New York: Thomas Crowell Company, 1976.

Carisella, P. J. and James W. Ryan. The Black Swallow of Death: The Incredible Story of Eugene Jacques Bullard, the World's First Black Combat Aviator. Massachusetts: Marlborough House, Inc., 1972.

Carson, Annette. Flight Fantastic: The Illustrated History of Aerobatics. England: Haynes Publishing Group, 1986.

Cheek, William and Aimee Lee. *John Mercer Langston and the Fight for Black Freedom 1829-65.* Chicago: University of Illinois Press, 1989.

"Chicago Colored Girl is Made Aviatrix By French." *Chicago Tribune,* 28 September 1921: N. pag.

"Chicago Colored Girl Learns to Fly Abroad." *Aerial Age Weekly.* 17 October 1921: 125.

"Chicago Girl Is a Full-Fledged Aviatrix Now." *The Chicago Defender* 1 October 1921: 1.

"Chicago Negro Aviatrix Back in U. S. from France." *Chicago Tribune* 26 September 1921: N. pag.

Cole, Johnnetta Betsch. Letter to Dr. Elizabeth Hadley Freydberg. 25 March 1992.

Coleman, Bessie. Letter to Norman Studios. 3 February 1926. Black Film Center Archive. Indiana University, Bloomington.

Coleman, Bessie. Letter to Mr. Norman. 23 February 1926. Black Film Center Archive. Indiana University, Bloomington.

Coleman, Marion. Personal Interview with Elizabeth Hadley Freydberg and Kathleen Collins. 12 January 1985.

---. Personal Interview with Elizabeth Hadley Freydberg. 19 March 1988.

Collier-Thomas, Bettye. *Black Women In America: Contributors to Our Heritage.* Washington, D. C.: The Bethune Museum-Archives, Inc., Institutions of the National Council of Negro Women, 1983.

"Colored Aviatrix Bobs Up Again." *Air Service News Letter.* Vol. 7. 20 February 1923: 4.

Corn, Joseph J. *The Winged Gospel: America's Romance with Aviation, 1900-1950.* New York: Oxford University Press, 1983.

Cripps, Thomas. *Slow Fade to Black: The Negro in American Film, 1900-1942.* New York: Oxford University Press, 1977.

Crisis, The: A Record of the Darker Races, Volumes 24-25, 1922-23: 74-75.

Cronon, E. David. *Black Moses: The Story of Marcus Garvey and the Universal Improvement Association*. 1955. Madison: The University of Wisconsin Press, 1969.

Cunard, Nancy. *Negro*. 1934. New York: Frederick Ungar Publishing Co., Inc., 1970.

Dada, Marsha A. "Drive Launched to Honor Coleman with Stamp." *The Chicago Defender* 5 May 1986:13.

Dalfiume, Richard M. *Desegregation of the U.S. Armed Forces*. Missouri: Unversity of Missouri Press, 1969.

Dance, Stanley. *The World of Earl Hines*. New York: Da Capo Press, Inc., 1977.

Davis, Marianna, ed. *Contributions of Black Women to America*. Vol. I. South Carolina: Kenday Press, Inc., 1982.

Dixon, Walter T. Jr. *The Negro in Aviation*. Baltimore: Clarke Press, 1950.

Donahey, Vic. Letter to Bessie Coleman. 27 August 1923. Black Film Center Archive. Indiana University, Bloomington.

Downs, Karl E. "Willa B. Brown: Vivacious Aviatrix." *Meet the Negro*. Pasadena, CA: The Login Press, 1943.

DuBois, W.E.B. *The Autobiography of W.E.B. Du Bois: A Soliloquy on Viewing My Life from the Last Decade of Its First Century*. New York: International Publishers, 1968.

Dunbar, Paul Laurence. "A Council of State." *The Strength of Gideon and Other Stories*. 1899. New York: Dodd Mead & Company, 1900. 315-338.

---. *The Complete Poems of Paul Laurence Dunbar*. 1940. New York: Dodd, Mead & Company, 1970.

Dwiggins, Don. *Hollywood Pilot: The Biography of Paul Mantz*. Foreword by Lowell Thomas. New York: Doubleday & Company, Inc., 1967.

Earhart, Amelia. *The Fun of It: Random Records of My Own Flying and of Women in Aviation*. Chicago: Academy Press Limited, 1977.

Erenberg, Lewis A. *Steppin' Out: New York Nightlife and the Transformation of American Culture, 1890-1930*. Chicago: The University of Chicago Press, 1981.

Farrell, Mary D. and Elizabeth Silverthorne. *First Ladies of Texas: The First One Hundred Years 1836-1936, A History*. Belton, Texas: Stillhouse Hollow Publishers, Inc., 1976.

Farmer, James H. *Broken Wings: Hollywood's Air Crashes*. Montana: Pictorial Histories Publishing Company, 1984.

Farmer, James H. *Celluloid Wings: The Impact of Movies on Aviation*. Pennsylvania: Tab Books Inc., 1984.

"Fatal Aeroplane Accident at Boston [Harriet Quimby]," *Science American*, 107:27. July 13, 1912.

Fine, Elsa Honig. *The Afro-American Artist: A Search for Identity.* New York: Holt, Rinehart and Winston, Inc., 1973.

"The 1st Black Woman flier," *Chicago Tribune* 8 May 1980.

Fitzgerald, Francis Scott, quoted by William Rose Benét. *The Readers's Encyclopedia.* 2nd ed. New York: Thomas Y. Crowell Company, 1965.

Fletcher, Winona L. "Georgia Douglas Johnson." *Dictionary of Literary Biography 51: Afro-American Writers from the Harlem Renaissance to 1940.* Eds. Trudier Harris and Thadious M. Davis. Detroit: Gale Research, 1987. 153-163.

Flexnor, Eleanor. *Century of Struggle: The Woman's Rights Movement in the United States.* 1959. Massachusetts: The Belknap Press of Harvard University Press, 1982.

"Florida Mayor Drinks Toast To 'Brave Bess,'" *The Chicago Defender,* May 5, 1926.

"Flying Free: Early Black Aviators Break the Color Barrier." *Paine: A Magazine for Alumni and Friends of the College.* Autumn 1986: 2+.

Fokker, Anthony H. G. and Bruce Gould. *Flying Dutchman: The Life of Anthony Fokker.* 1931. New York: Arno Press Inc., 1972.

Franklin, John Hope. *From Slavery to Freedom: A History of Negro Americans.* 3rd ed. New York: Alfred A. Knopf, 1968.

Freydberg, Elizabeth Hadley. "Nineteenth Century Euro-Cultural Influences in the Works of Three Black American Artists," 1984. Unpublished essay, received the 1984 National Council for Black Studies Scholastic Essay Award. North Carolina, 1984.

Gates, Henry Louis Jr. "An Interview with Josephine Baker and James Baldwin." *Afro-American Writing Today: An Anniversary Issue of the Southern Review.* Ed. James Olney. Louisiana: Louisiana State University Press, 1985. 8-16.

Giddings, Paula. *When and Where I Enter: The Impact of Black Women On Race and Sex in America.* New York: William and Company, Inc., 1984.

"Gigantic Klonvocation Knights and Ladies of the Ku Klux Klan." *Columbus Dispatch* 2 September 1923: 38.

Goddard, Chris. "Theater and Dance." *Jazz Away from Home.* New York: Paddington Press, Ltd., 1979.

Goodlett, Helen. "Waxahachie, Texas." *The Handbook of Texas.* Ed. Walter Prescott Welch. Vol. 2. Austin: The Texas State Historical Association, 1952. 871-72.

"The Good Will Fliers in the West Indies," *Tuskegee Messenger,* X Dec. 1934: 3.

"Granted Pilots License [Dorothy Darby, Parachute Jumper]," *The Chicago Defender,* 21 May 1938:1.

Green, Barbara-Marie. "Bessie Coleman First Black Aviatrix--A 'Woman With A Dream.'" *New York Voice.* 20 October 1984: 13.

Grimsted, David. *Melodrama Unveiled: American Theater and Culture 1800-1850.* Chicago: The University of Chicago Press, 1968.

---. "*Uncle Tom* From Page to Stage: Limitations of Nineteenth-Century Drama." *The Quarterly Journal of Speech.* October 1970: 235-244.

"Guardsmen to Bury Chicago Aviatrix." *Chicago Tribune* 5 May 1926.

Hansberry, Lorraine. *A Raisin in the Sun: Expanded Twenty-fifth Anniversary Edition and The Sign in Sidney Brustein's Window.* 1958. New York: New American Library, 1987.

"Harlem's Newest Apartments Named After Black 'Joan of Arc.'" *The New York News* 23 July 1927: N. pag.

Harmon Bragg, Janet. Telephone interview with Elizabeth Hadley Freydberg. 8 April 1988.

Harris, Sherwood. *The First to Fly: Aviations's Pioneer Days.* New York: Simon and Schuster, 1970.

Harrison, Daphne Duval. *Black Pearls: Blues Queens of the 1920s.* New Brunswick: Rutgers University Press, 1988.

Hart, Phillip. Telephone interview with Elizabeth Hadley Freydberg. 21 May 1988.

Haskins, James. *Black Dance in America: A History Through It's People.* New York: Harper/Collins Publishers, 1990.

---. *Black Theater in America.* New York: Thomas Y. Crowell, 1982.

---. *The Cotton Club: A Pictorial and Social History of the Most Famous Symbol of the Jazz Era.* London: Robson Books, 1985.

Hatch, James V., ed. *Black Theater, U. S. A.: Forty-Five Plays By Black Americans 1847-1974.* New York: The Free Press, 1974.

---. "Some African Influences on the Afro-American Theatre." Ed. Errol Hill. *The Theatre of Black Americans: A Collection of Critical Essays.* 1980. New York: Applause Theatre Book Publishers, 1987.

Hatlen, Theodore W. *Orientation to the Theater.* 2nd ed. New York: Appleton-Century-Crofts, 1972.

Hemenway, Robert E. *Zora Neale Hurston: A Literary Biography.* Chicago: University of Illinois Press, 1977.

Henri, Florette. *Black Migration: Movement North 1900-1920.* New York: Anchor Books, 1976.

Heritage, John. *The Wonderful World of Aircraft.* London: Octopus Books Limited, 1980.

Hill, Erroll. *Black Heroes: Seven Plays.* New York: Applause Theatre Book Publishers, Inc., 1989.

---. "From Artist to Activist," *Shakespeare in Sable: A History of Black Shakespearean Actors.* Amherst: The University of Massachusetts Press, 1984. 64-78.

---. *The Theatre of Black Americans: A Collection of Critical Essays.* 1980. New York: Applause Theatre Book Publishers, 1987.

Hodgman, Ann and Rudy Djabbaroff. *Sky-Stars: The History of Women in Aviation.* New York: Atheneum, 1981.

"How Integration Has Worked in the Arm [sic] Forces," *Sepia,* December 1959, 14-17.

Hughes, Langston. *The Big Sea: An Autobiography.* 1940. New York: Hill and Wang, 1981.

---. "Black Influences in the American Theater: I." *The Black American Reference Book.* Ed. Mabel M. Smythe. New Jersey: Prentice-Hall, Inc., 1976. 684-704.

Hughes, Langston and Milton Meltzer. *Black Magic: A Pictorial History of Black Entertainers in America.* New York: Bonanza Books, 1967.

Hughes, Langston. *Fight for Freedom: The Story of the NAACP.* New York: W. W. Norton & Company, Inc., 1962.

---. *I Wonder As I wander.* New York, 1956.

---. "When Harlem Was in Vogue." *Town and Country* July 1940: 64-66.

---. "The Negro Artist and the Racial Mountain." *The Nation* 23 June 1926: 692-694.

Hull, Gloria T. *Color, Sex, and Poetry: Three Women Writers of the Harlem Renaissance.* Bloomington: Indiana University Press, 1987.

Hunt, Rufus A. *The Coffey Intersection.* Chicago: J.R.D.B. Enterprises, 1982.

---. "Bessie Coleman--The World's First Black Female Pilot."

International Forest Of Friendship, The. Official Commemoration Certificate 19 July 1986. Atchison, Kansas.

Johnson, James Weldon. *Along This Way.* New York, 1968.

---. *Black Manhattan.* 1930. New York: Arno Press and The New York Times, 1968.

Jourdain, E. B. Jr. "Bessie Coleman, Aviatrix Killed: Two Lives Snuffed Out When Plane Crashes Down." *The Chicago Defender* 8 May 1926: 1+.

Kelley, Robert. *The Shaping of the American Past.* 4th ed. 2 vols. New Jersey: Prentice-Hall, Inc., 1986.

Kelly, John. "Those Barnstorming Women." *The Sun* 9 April 1984: N. Pag.

Kimball, Robert, and William Bolcom. *Reminiscing with Sissle and Blake.* New York: Viking Press, 1973.

King, Anita. "Brave Bessie: First Black Pilot, Part I," *Essence Magazine,* May 1976: 36.

---. "Brave Bessie: First Black Pilot, Part II," *Essence Magazine,* June 1976: 48.

"Klan Initiates 2300 at Monday Meeting." *Columbus Dispatch* 4 September 1923: 18.

Klotman, Phyllis Rauch. *Frame by Frame: A Black Filmography.* Bloomington: Indiana University Press, 1979.

Kraditor, Aileen. *The Ideas of the Women Suffrage Movement, 1899-1929.* New York: Anchor Books/Doubledy, 1971.

Kriz, Marjorie. "Bessie Coleman, Aviation Pioneer," *U. S. Department of Transportation News.* U. S. Department of Transportation Federal Aviation Administration Office of Public Affairs, Great Lakes Region, n.d.

Kriz, Marjorie. "They Had Another Dream: Blacks Took to the Air Early," *U. S. Department of Transportation News.* Reprinted from *FAA World,* January 1980. N. Pag.

"Latest Bulletins, Woman Flyer Reaches New York [Bessie Coleman]," *The Afro-American* 30 September 1921: 1.

"Lest We Forget: Bessie Coleman (1893-1926)," *Bilalian News* 24 August 1979: 11+.

Levering-Lewis, David. *When Harlem Was In Vogue.* New York: Alfred A. Knopf, 1981.

Levine, Lawrence W. *Black Culture and Black Consciousness: Afro-American Folk Thought from Slavery to Freedom.* New York: Oxford University Press, 1977.

---. *Highbrow Lowbrow: The Emergence of Cultural Hierarchy in America.* Massachusetts: Cambridge University Press, 1988.

Lieb, Sandra R. *Mother of the Blues: A Study of Ma Rainey.* Massachusetts: The University of Massachusetts Press, 1981.

Locke, Alain *The New Negro.* 1925. New York: Atheneum, 1980.

Lomax, Judy. "The Good Old Crazy Days in America." *Women of the Air.* New York: Dodd, Mead and Company, 1987. 24-36; "Amelia Earhart: America's Winged Legend," 68-83.

MacCracken, Wm. P. Jr., Assistant Secretary of Commerce for Aeronautics. Letter to Oscar C. Brown, Cooperative Business, Professional and Labor League. 26 May 1928. Record Group 237, Federal Aviation Administration, Central Files. National Archives and Records Administration: Washington, DC.

MacGregor, Morris J. Jr. *Integration of the Armed Forces 1940-1965.* Washington, D.C.: U. S. Government Printing Office, 1980.

Manning, Patrick and James S. Speigler. "Kojo Tovalou-Houenou: Franco-Dahomean Patriot." Unpublished essay, presented at the African Studies Association. Chicago, November 1988.

McDowell, Barbara and Hana Umlauf. "Women Aloft," *The Good Housekeeping Woman's Almanac.* New York: Newspaper Enterprise Association, Inc., 1977. 369-371.

McDuffie, Ruby Mae. Letter to Bessie Coleman. 29 April 1926. "Chicago Pays Parting Tribute to 'Brave Bessie' Coleman." By Evangeline Roberts. *The Chicago Defender* 15 May 1926: 2.

McKay, Claude. *Harlem: Negro Metropolis.* New York: Harcourt Brace Jovanovich, Inc., 1968.

Meserve, Walter J. "An Age of Melodrama: Sensation and Sententia 1850-1912." *The Revels History of Drama in English, American Drama.* Eds. Travis Bogard, T. W. Craik, Richard Moody, and Walter J. Meserve. Vol. 8. New York: Barnes and Noble Books, 1977. 194-202.

---. *An Outline History of American Drama.* New Jersey: Littlefield, Adams & Co., 1965.

"[Miss Bessie Coleman, a Librarian]," *The Half-Century Magazine: A Colored Magazine for the Home and Homemaker.* November, 1921: 6.

"The Monument to Bessie Coleman." *The New York News* 30 July 1927: N. pag.

Morrissey, Muriel Earhart and Carol L. Osborne. *Amelia, My Courageous Sister: Biography of Amelia Earhart, True Facts About Her Disappearance.* California: Osborne Publisher, Incoroporated, 1987.

Moskos, Charles C. Jr. "Racial Integration in the Armed Forces." *The Making of Black America.* Eds. August Meier and Elliot Rudwick. Vol. 2. New York: Atheneum Press, 1969.

Mosley, Leonard. *Lindbergh: A Biography.* New York: Doubleday and Company, Inc., 1976.

Motley, Constance Baker. "The Legal Status of the Black American." *The Black American Reference Book.* Ed. Mabel M. Smythe. New Jersey: Prentice-Hall, Inc., 1976. 90-127.

"Negress in Flying Show: Bessie Coleman to Give Exhibition for Fifteenth Regiment." *The New York Times* 27 August 1922: 2.

"Negress Pilots Airplane: Bessie Coleman Makes Three Flights for Fifteenth Infantry," *The New York Times* 4 September 1922: 9.

"Negro Aviatrix Arrives: Bessie Coleman Flew Planes of Many Types in Europe." *New York Times* 14 August 1922: 4.

"Negro Aviatrix to Tour the Country." *Air Service News Letter.* Vol. 5. 1 November 1921: 11.

Norman, Richard. Letter to D. Ireland Thomas. 19 January 1926. Black Film Center Archive. Indiana University, Bloomington.

Nugent, John Peer. *The Black Eagle.* New York: Stein and Day Publishers, 1971.

Orlando Morning Sentinel 1 May 1926: 8.

Ottley, Roi. *The Lonely Warrior: The Life and Times of Robert S. Abbott.* Chicago: Henry Regnery Company, 1955.

---. *New World A-Coming.* 1943. New York: Arno Press and The New York Times, 1968.

Patterson, Elois Coleman. *Memoirs of the Late Bessie Coleman Aviatrix: Pioneer of the Negro People in Aviation.* Elois Coleman Patterson, 1969.

Patterson, Zella J. Black. *Langston University: A History.* Oklahoma: University of Oklahoma Press, 1979.

Pendo, Stephen. *Aviation in the Cinema.* New Jersey: The Scarecrow Press, Inc., 1985.

Perrett, Geoffrey. *America in the Twenties: A History.* New York: Simon & Schuster, Inc., 1982.

Placksin, Sally. "Alberta Hunter." *American Women in Jazz: 1900 to the Present Their Words, Lives, and Music.* New York: Wideview Books, 1982. 36-39; "Lil Hardin Armstrong." 58-63.

Planck, Charles E. *Women with Wings.* New York: Harper & Brothers Publishers, 1942.

"Plans Flight [Miss Bessie Coleman]." *The Chicago Defender* 22 September 1923: 2.

Poindexter, Blaine. "Bessie Coleman Makes Initial Aerial Flight: Chicagoans See Girl Who Flew Over Berlin in Series of Stunts." *The Chicago Defender* 21 October 1922: 3.

Powell, William J. *Black Wings.* Los Angeles: Ivan Deach Publishing Company, 1934.

"Rain Halts the Initial Flight of Miss Bessie," *The Chicago Defender* 2 September, 1922: 9.

Rampersad, Arnold. *The Life of Langston Hughes: I, Too, Sing America.* Vol. I, 1902-1941. New York: Oxford University Press, 1986.

Ramsaye, Terry. "The Screen and Press Conspire." *A Million and One Nights: A History of the Motion Picture.* 1926. New York: Simon and Schuster, 1964. 652-669.

Roach, Hildred. *Black American Music: Past and Present.* Boston: Crescendo Publishing Co., 1973.

Roberts, Evangeline. "Chicago Pays Parting Tribute to 'Brave Bessie' Coleman." *The Chicago Defender* 15 May 1926: 2.

Rose, Al. *Eubie Blake.* New York: Schirmer Books, A Division of Macmillan Publishing Co., Inc., 1979.

Roseberry, C. R. *The Challenging Skies: The Colorful Story of Aviation's Most Exciting Years, 1919-1939.* New York: Doubleday and Company, Inc., 1966.

Rudwick, Elliot. *W. E. B. DuBois: Voice of the Black Protest Movement.* Chicago: University of Illinois Press, 1960.

St. Laurent, Philip. "Bessie Coleman, Aviator." The Negro In World History/Part 70. *Washington Sunday Star Tuesday Magazine.* January 1973: N. Pag.

"Salute to a Nervy Lady [Bessie Coleman]," *Chicago Tribune* 8 May 1980: N. pag.

Sampson, Henry T. *Blacks in Blackface: A Source Book on Early Black Musical Shows*. New Jersey: The Scarecrow Press, Inc., 1980.

Sandburg, Carl. *The Chicago Race Riots: July, 1919*. 1919, 1947. New York: Harcourt, Brace & World, Inc., 1969.

Scott, Emmett J. *Official History of the American Negro in the World War*. 1919. New York: Arno Press, 1969.

Semple, E. A. "America's First Woman Aviator [Harriet Quimby]," *Overland*, n. s. pors., 58:525-32; December 1911.

Shafer, Yvonne. "Black Actors in the Nineteenth Century American Theatre." *CLA Journal, XX* (March, 1977), 387-400.

Sharratt, Bernard. "The Politics of the Popular?--From Melodrama to Television." *Performance and Politics in Popular Drama: Aspects of Popular Entertainment in Theatre, Film and Television 1800-1976*. Eds. David Bradby, Louis James, and Bernard Sharratt. New York: Cambridge University Press, 1980. 275-295.

Shaw, Dale. *Titans of the American Stage: Edwin Forrest, the Booths, the O'Neills*. Philadelphia: The Westminster Press, 1971.

Shepperd, Gladys Byram. *Mary Church Terrell Respectable Person*. Baltimore: Human Relations Press, 1959.

Shockley, Ann Allen. *Afro-American Women Writers 1746-1933: An Anthology and Critical Guide*. New York: New American Library, 1988.

"'Shuffle Along' Company Gives Fair Flyer Cup," *The Chicago Defender* 8 October 1921: 2.

Slide, Anthony. *The Vaudevillians: A Dictionary of Vaudeville Performers*. Connecticut: Arlington House, 1981.

Southern, Eileen. *The Music of Black Americans: A History*. 1971. New York: W.W.Norton and Company, 1983.

Spear, Allan H. *Black Chicago: The Making of A Negro Ghetto*. Chicago: The University of Chicago Press, 1967.

Spencer, Chauncey E. *Who Is Chauncey Spencer?* Detroit: Broadside Press, 1975.

Stearns, Marshall and Jean. *Jazz Dance*. New York: Macmillan Publishing Co. Inc., 1968.

Sterling, Dorothy. "Ida B. Wells: Voice of a People." *Black Foremothers: Three Lives*. New York: The Feminist Press, 1979. 60-117.

---. "Washerwomen, Maumas, Exodusters, Jubileers." *We Are Your Sisters: Black Women in the Nineteenth Century*. New York: W. W. Norton and Company, 1984. 355-394.

Terborg-Penn, Rosalyn. "Discrimination Against Afro-American Women in the Women's Movement, 1830-1920," *The Afro-*

American Woman: Struggles and Images. Eds. Sharon Harley and Rosalyn Terborg-Penn. New York: Kennikat Press, 1978.

Terrell, Mary Church. *A Colored Woman in a White World*. Washington, D.C.: Ransdell Inc. Publishers, 1940.

Terry, Wallace. "Black Soldiers and Vietnam." *The Black American: A Documentary History*. Ed. Leslie H. Fishel, Jr. and Benjamin Quarles. New York: William Morrow and Co., 1970.

"Texas Negro Girl Becomes Able Aviatrix." *Houston Post Dispatch* 7 May 1925: 4.

"They Take to The Sky: Group of Midwest Women Follow Path Blazed by Pioneer Bessie Coleman." *Ebony* May 1977: 89-96.

Thomas, James J. Letter to Bessie Coleman. 27 August 1923. Black Film Center Archive. Indiana University, Bloomington.

Toll, Robert C. *Blacking Up: The Minstrel Show in Nineteenth-Century America*. New York: Oxford University Press, 1974.

---. *On With the Show: The First Century of Show Business in America*. New York: Oxford University Press, 1976.

---. *The Entertainment Machine: American Show Business in the Twentieth Century*. New York: Oxford University Press, 1982.

"To Hold Funeral For Negro Aviatrix," *Orlando Morning Sentinel* 3 May 1926:5.

Toppin, Edgar A. *A Biographical History of Blacks in America Since 1528*. New York: David McKay Company, Inc., 1971.

Travis, Dempsey J. *An Autobiography of Black Chicago*. Chicago: Urban Research Institute,Inc., 1981.

Turner, Darwin. *Black Drama In America: An Anthology*. Conneticut: Fawcett Publications, Inc., 1971.

"U.S. Armed Forces: 1950; record of Negro Integration in the services since President Truman's executive order," *Our World*, June 1951, 11-35.

Van Vechten, Carl. *"KeepA-Inchin' Along": Selected Writings of Carl Van Vechten About Black Art and Letters*. Ed. Bruce Kellner. Connecticut: Greenwood Press, 1979.

---. *Nigger Heaven*, New York: Alfred A. Knopf, 1926.

Villard, Henry Serrano. *Contact! The Story of The Early Birds*. New York: Thomas Y. Crowell Company, 1968.

Vincent, Theodore G. *Black Power and the Garvey Movement* (San Francisco: Ramparts Press, 1976).

Von Hardesty and Dominick Pisano, *Black Wings: The American Black in Aviation*. Washington, D.C.: National Air And Space Museum, 1983.

Ward, Theodore. *Big White Fog*. Hatch, *Black Theater*. 281-319.

Washington, Mary J. "A Race Soars Upward," *Opportunity, A Journal of Negro Life*, XII (Oct. 1934), 301.

Waterford, Janet Harmon [Bragg]. "Race Interest In Aviation In Actuality Begins With Advent of Bessie Coleman." *The Chicago Defender* 28 March 1936: 1.

Waters, Enoch P. "Black Wings Over America," unid. clip. in "Aviators and Aviation" file, Schomburg Collection, New York Public Library.

---. "Little Air Show Becomes A National Crusade." *American Diary: A Personal History of the Black Press*. Chicago: Path Press, Inc., 1987. 195-210.

---. Personal Interview with Elizabeth Hadley Freydberg and Kathleen Collins. 12 January 1985.

Waters, Ethel, with Charles Samuels. *His Eye Is on the Sparrow*. New York: Doubleday and Company, 1950.

Wells, Ida B. *A Red Record: Tabulated Statistics and Alleged Causes of Lynchings in the United States, 1892-1893-1894*. New York: Arno Press, 1971.

---. *Crusade for Justice: The Autobiography of Ida B. Wells-Barnett*. Ed. Alfreda M. Duster. Chicago: The University of Chicago Press, 1970.

White, Walter. *Fire in the Flint*. New York: Knopf, 1924.

Williams, Fannie Barrier. "The Club Movement Among Colored Women of America." *A New Negro for a New Century: An Accurate and Up-To-Date Record of the Upward Struggles of the Negro Race*. Eds. Booker T. Washington, N. B. Wood, and Fannie Barrier Williams. 1900. New York: Arno Press and The New York Times, 1969. 378-428.

Wilson, Garff B. *Three Hundred Years of American Drama and Theatre: From Ye Bare and Ye Cubb to Hair*. New Jersey: Prentice Hall, Inc., 1973.

Woll, Allen. *Black Musical Theatre: From Coontown to Dreamgirls*. Baton Rouge: Louisiana State University Press, 1989.

Woodward, C. Vann. *The Strange Career of Jim Crow*. 3rd ed. New York: Oxford University Press, 1974.

Wright, Richard. *Native Son*. New York: Harper & Brothers Publishers, 1940.

Wright, Richard and Paul Green. *Native Son*. Hatch, *Black Theater* 394-431.

"Young Aviatrix To Teach Air-Minded Billikens The Principles of Aviation [Willa Brown]." *The Chicago Defender*, 16 May 1936: 15.

Young, David and Neal Callahan. *Fill the Heavens With Commerce: Chicago Aviation 1855-1926*. Chicago: Chicago Review Press, 1981.

"Young Woman Flyer Gets Pilots License: Willa Brown, Chicago Aviatrix, Can Carry Passengers, Give Instructions or Make Cross-Country Flights," *Pittsburgh Courier,* 2 July 1938: 11+.

INDEX